the

WESTERN

ísles

guíoe Book

by CHARLES TAIT

na h-eíleanan an íar

ISBN 09517859 3 1

The Western Isles Guide Book
copyright Charles Tait 2002
Published by Charles Tait photographic
Kelton, St Ola, Orkney KW15 1TR
Tel 01856 873738 Fax 01856 875313
charles.tait@zetnet.co.uk
www.charles-tait.co.uk

This book is dedicated to the memory of
my step-mother, Jean Maxwell Tait

Text, design and layout copyright Charles
Tait, all photographs copyright Charles Tait
unless otherwise credited, old photographs
from Charles Tait collection
Maps reproduced from Ordnance Survey
mapping with permission of the Controller
of HMSO, Crown Copyright Reserved MC
100035677 where credited.
Printing by Nevisprint Ltd, Fort William

ISBN 09517859 3 1

Front cover: Bagh Steinige, Scarista, Harris
This page: Sunset at Halaman Bay, Barra

the
western isles

guide book

by CHARLES TAIT

na h-eileanan an iar

hebudes

sudreyar

innse gall

outer hebrides

CONTENTS

The Standing Stones at Callanish are dramatically sited on a ridge overlooking Loch Roag

The **Western Isles** is a chain of over 200 islands to the west of Northern Scotland which stretches 200km (130 miles) from the **Butt of Lewis** in the north (58⁰31'N, 6⁰16'W) to **Barra Head** (56⁰46'N, 7⁰39'W) in the south. The islands are between 50km (30 miles) and 100km (60 miles) from the Scottish Mainland across the Minch and the Sea of the Hebrides and cover about 2,900km² (1,118 miles²).

The islands were referred to by Scottish Gaels as *Innse Gall* - Islands of Strangers - the Norsemen. They are also called the **Outer Hebrides** - "Hebrides" probably arose from the Greek *"Hebudes"* by mis-transciption. Today the Gaelic influence remains strong, but Norse is still evident in many of the place-names. About 27,000 people inhabit 12 of the islands, with the majority of the popula-tion living in Lewis (22,000). The main town and ferry port is Stornoway with a population of about 8,000.

From Scotland the Western Isles appear as a long series of hilltops on the horizon, and when approached from the east they at first seem rocky and bleak, with many inlets and small rocky islands. In contrast, on the west side there are many sandy beach-es and attractive bays, with rela-tively few high cliffs.

Communications with Mainland Scotland are very good. The *Isle of Lewis* runs between Stornoway and Ullapool, while The *Hebrides* connects Tarbert in Harris with Uig in Skye and Lochmaddy in North Uist. In the south, the *Clansman* links Lochboisdale in South Uist and Castlebay in Barra with Oban. Scalpay is connected to Harris by a bridge, while Eriskay, Berneray and Vatersay have causeways now. There is a ferry link between Harris and North Uist, and also from South Uist to Barra. Air links with Inverness and Glasgow and an inter-island air service are run by British Airways Express. Highland Airways operates services to Inverness.

Although the earliest written ref-erences to the islands are proba-bly in the Norse sagas, which date from the 12th century, it is possible that Pytheas the Greek may have visited Lewis around 325BC during his voyage, when he established the latitude of the Stornoway area. It was not until the late 17th century, however, that detailed accounts began to be made about visits to the area. In more recent times many emi-nent people have visited the Western Isles and a number have written in various terms about their experiences.

There are a number of distinguished local authors, and there is always a good selection of local books available in the bookshops, many in Gaelic. The library in Stornoway has a good reference section for those wishing to consult the many books which are "out of print".

The purpose of this Guide is to help visitors to the islands appreciate the Western Isles and enjoy their time here to the full. The idea is that the reader can assimilate information without effort and yet rapidly find out what he or she would most like to see and do, depending on interest, season or weather. There are so many things to see and do that a lifetime is not long enough!

Although the landscape is beautiful, history everywhere, and wildlife to rival anywhere on Earth, there is another aspect of the islands which is perhaps the most important and rewarding to get to know - the local people themselves. They are a friendly, hospitable people, mindful and respectful of their past and at the same time go-ahead and industrious. Do not hesitate to ask the

The North Ford, Oitir Mhòr, separates North Uist from Benbecula

way, or about things - you are sure to get a courteous reply - and if you are lucky you might get a few good stories as well! There is a saying in the Western Isles that *"When God made time he made plenty of it"*, which describes the apparent pace of life in the islands rather well.

A good map is a great help on all such visits and the Tourist Board produces a useful one on a scale of 1:125,000. The Ordnance Survey 1:50,000 series covers the Western Isles in six sheets, and is recommended for all serious explorers. While many of the places mentioned in this book are signposted, many are not, and OS references are thus given for many sites of interest.

COUNTRYSIDE CODE

We are justly proud of our historic sites, wildlife and environment. Please help ensure that future visitors may enjoy them as much as you by observing these guidelines:

1. Always use stiles and gates and close gates after you.
2. Always ask permission before entering agricultural land.
3. Keep to paths and take care to avoid fields of grass and crops.
4. Do not disturb livestock.
5. Take your litter away with you and do not light fires.
6. Do not pollute water courses or supplies.
7. Never disturb nesting birds.
8. Do not pick wild flowers or dig up plants.
9. Drive and park with due care and attention - do not obstruct or endanger others.
10. Always take care near cliffs and beaches - particularly with children and pets. Many beaches are dangerous for swimmers.
11. Walkers should take adequate clothes, wear suitable footwear and tell someone of their plans.
12. Above all please respect the life of the countryside - leave only footprints, take only photographs and pleasant memories.

Notice: While most of the sites of interest are open to the public and have marked access, many are on private land. No right of access is implied in the description, and if in doubt it is always polite to ask. Also, while many roads and tracks are rights of way, not all are.

The Calmac ferry "Clansman" passing Kisimul Castle, Barra

A Tour of the Main Ancient Sites

There are so many sites of interest in the Western Isles that it would take a lifetime to visit them all. However even on a short visit it is possible to take in human constructions from a wide range of periods.

The early settlers have left much evidence behind them, ranging from numerous chambered cairns, such as the well-preserved example at Langass on North Uist, or the enigmatic Steinicleit at Shader in Lewis to the spectacular standing stone circles at Callanish.

Neolithic, Bronze Age, Iron Age, Norse, Medieval and more modern sites are scattered from the north of Lewis to Barra Head. While some are signposted, most are not, making maps essential in many cases.

Perhaps the most dramatic of all the Western Isles monuments are the Standing Stones at Callanish. These megaliths and the adjacent smaller circles represent an immense amount of work for a Neolithic society and were clearly erected with a strong purpose.

Dun Carloway is the best-preserved of the many Iron Age brochs and duns in the islands. This broch has survived despite being used as a quarry for nearby blackhouses and shows the galleried structure typical of all brochs.

Langass chambered cairn, North Uist

Steinicleit, West Lewis

Standing Stones of Callanish

The well-preserved broch of Dun Carloway

Duns and brochs form a class of domestic structure often termed as "Atlantic Roundhouses". There are many throughout the islands, but the best are probably in North Uist, especially Dun Sticir, near Otternish and Dun Torcuill.

Dun Torcuill, North Uist

Usually situated on islets on lochs and accessed by causeways, these structures were often occupied for long periods.

There are only a few remaining castles in the islands, and Kisimul Castle on Barra is the most dramatic. There was also a castle at Stornoway which was largely destroyed by Cromwell's troops, and finally by the building of the ferry pier.

Kisimul Castle, Castlebay, Barra

The Western Isles have many ancient church and monastic sites. The best preserved is the 16th century St Clement's Church at Rodel, Harris, but there are many more to visit.

St Clement's Church, Rodel, South Harris

Blackhouses were the standard domestic building until the 19th century throughout Scotland. These seemingly primitive dwellings had thatched roofs, and a central fireplace. The smoke escaped through a hole in the roof, and the human inhabitants shared their roof with their livestock, much as in Neolithic times. The houses were warm and well suited to the climate, if rather basic.

Blackhouse museum, Arnol, West Lewis

Nature and Environment

The environment of the Western Isles is the result of geology, climate, glaciation, plants and animals, including man, over time. The rocks are mostly ancient gneiss which is one of the oldest rocks on Earth. The sea plays a very important part in the shaping of an island environment and this is very apparent here where the coastline extends to about 2,100km (approx 1,300 miles).

Mingulay from the west

The islands have several distinct types of terrain. These include moorland and hills, machair, sandy beaches and dunes, rocky coasts and cliffs, woodlands and inland lochs. Much of the interior of the islands, especially Lewis, comprises vast areas of peatland, while the eastern seaboard is mostly rocky. In contrast the western coasts are mostly sandy beaches, backed by machair and dunes, with some low rocky cliffs in places..

Peatbank in summer, North Uist

Spectacular sandy beaches dominate the western sides of the islands, and windblown sand has accumulated in large quantities resulting in large areas of machair, which when fertilised with seaweed and manure, makes excellent agricultural soil. The only sandy beaches on the east side are north of Stornoway and on Benbecula, as well as on some of the outlying islands.

Wildflowers on the machair, Barra

Loch Seaforth from the east

Long fiord-like sea lochs indent much of the east coast of the islands. The biggest of these, Loch Seaforth, is one of many such drowned valleys which have been sculpted by glaciers. These coasts are mostly rocky, with many small islands and

skerries. The thin, acid soils are not very fertile and deposits of peat are limited.

Inland, especially in Lewis and the Uists the terrain is dotted with hundreds of lochs, large and small. These have formed in hollows scooped out by glaciers and afford excellent trout fishing.

Lochmaddy from the North Lee

The Western Isles are thought to have had their own relatively thin ice cap in the last glaciation, and were one of the first areas to be ice free, around 10,000 years ago. One of the results of this is that whereas much of mainland Scotland has risen since the melting of the ice, the Western Isles have actually sunk. Combined with the rise in sea level this means that much land area has been lost to the sea.

Uig Bay at high tide from Crowlista

The climate of the Western Isles is essentially oceanic, and is controlled by the North Atlantic weather systems. Most of the year this means that a series of depressions crosses the area, with their attendant wind and rain, but anticyclones can also last for weeks once established. Rainfall is relatively low, but average wind speed is high.

Manish, on the Golden Road, East Harris

Tràigh Mhòr, Barra - site of the only beach airfield in UK

The temperature of the sea ranges from a minimum of 7 degrees in January to a maximum of 14 degrees in August. This means that Summers are cool, and Winters mild. All of the landscape is exposed to the prevailing salt-laden westerly wind, which inhibits the growth of trees and shrubs except in specially sheltered locations.

Nature and Environment

Atlantic Puffin - very numerous on offshore islands

The Western Isles are home to a large number of birds and sea mammals. Most of the large colonies of sea birds are however on inaccessible outlying islands, such as St Kilda, the Flannans, the Shiants, Sula Sgeir and Rona.

Some of the best opportunities for seabird (and cetacean) watching are to be had from the various ferry crossings from the Mainland or between the islands, and the Sounds of Harris and Barra are particularly good places for the binoculars.

In general the car is an ideal hide as so many species will completely ignore vehicles,

Oystercatcher

but will instantly depart as soon as the observer leaves his or her car. It always pays to keep a weather eye open for wildlife while driving in the Western Isles.

Dunlin

Golden Eagles may be seen throughout the islands, as can Merlin, Peregrine and Buzzard and the occasional Hen Harrier or Short-eared Owl in the Uists where there are Voles. Sea Eagles, which breed on Rum, are also sometimes around.

The Corncrake remains locally common in the Uists and Barra, and the rasping call of the males is a feature of the meadows in summer. They are hard to see, as they tend to hide in vegetation and can throw their calls which makes them very hard to locate.

The extensive flat sandy beaches, and mud flats especially in the Uists attract an internationally important population of waders, while the many lochs hold a lot of ducks, geese and divers. Near Stornoway the extensive sand and mud flats area of the Sands of Tong is one of the best places for waders and waterfowl.

Seabirds make up the largest number of breeding birds in the area. There are huge colonies of Gannets at St Kilda and Sula Sgeir. These spectacular birds may be seen plunge diving off all of

Gannets breed on offshore islands

the coasts. Puffins and other auks are also common, and may be seen from the ferries, but only breed on offshore islands. Great and Arctic Skuas also breed, along with large numbers of Arctic Terns and a few Little Terns.

The woodland around Lews Castle in Stornoway is home to a large number of passerines, otherwise mostly absent from the area. The walks in these woods afford many opportunities to view these species. Dippers breed near the Creed and Bayhead Rivers near Stornoway.

There is an RSPB Reserve and visitor centre at Balranald on North Uist which is an excellent place to view the species which breed on the machair lochs.

birdwatcher as a large variety of species may be viewed within a relatively small area.

The outliers - the Monach Islands, St Kilda, the Flannans, Sula Sgeir, Rona, the Shiant Islands and the southern Barra Isles are the best places to view breeding seabirds. Although St Kilda has the biggest such colonies, all of these islands offer spectacular opportunities for bird watching.

During Spring and Autumn the islands are in the path of migrants which breed in the Arctic and many unusual vagrants can turn up. During migration times there are many good vantage sites for sea watching, especially the Butt of Lewis, Tiumpan Head and on South Uist, Rubha Ardvule. Perhaps the best vantage points are however from the ferries.

Arctic Tern

The rare Leach's Petrel breeds on Hirta and on Rona

Guillemot

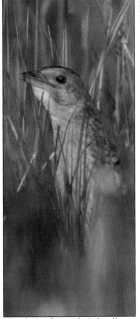

The elusive Corncrake is locally common on the Uists and Barra

There is also a National Nature Reserve at Loch Druidibeg on South Uist, which holds large numbers of breeding Greylag Geese.

In the Uists the unique combination of coast, machair, croftlands, moorland and mountain offers much to the

Golden Eagles breed throughout the Isles and are seen quite often

The sandy soil of the machair is carpeted with wild flowers in the summer

The diverse habitats of the Western Isles, which include acidic, bare gneiss rocks, peat-covered moorland, sandy beaches backed by fertile machair, rocky coasts, inland lochs and bogs, woodland and cultivated croftland, has allowed a similarly diverse flora to proliferate.

Trees only survive when protected from grazing and when sheltered

In summer the machair areas are covered by a carpet of wild flowers - with up to 45 different species per square metre. In early summer whites and yellows predominate, while later reds, blues and purples take over. Orchids, some of which only occur in the Hebrides, are particularly common during the summer.

Sandy shores also support many species. Sea Rocket and Scurvy Grass are widespread while the dunes have largely been stabilised with Marram grass.

Inland, the cultivated "black-

land" between the machair and the moorland, with fields for pasture and hay also supports a wide variety of wild flowers, especially when reseeding has not been done recently, and when the crop is cut late in the season.

The moors are covered with peat, often several feet deep, but Heather, mosses, Sundew, Bog Asphodel and Cotton Grass add colour during the summer. Peat forms when rainwater does not drain away, resulting in a very high water table. This prevents breakdown of plant material, which builds up to form peat.

Although there are few areas of natural woodland today there is evidence that trees were more widespread in the past. Many stumps of trees have been found underneath peat cuttings, suggesting that climate change to wetter conditions, and the resulting growth of peat engulfed the trees.

The legend is that the Vikings

Much of the landscape in Lewis and North Uist is covered with peatbog

burnt all the trees but it is more likely that cutting for fuel and timber combined with the grazing of domestic animals preventing regeneration wiped out most of the woodland. Small islands on sheltered lochs are nearly always covered with trees and bushes, suggesting that protection from sheep and deer would allow woodland to thrive in some places.

Sea Rocket covers the top of the beach at Kilphedar, South Uist

The only large area of woodland is around Lews Castle at Stornoway. However this was planted in the mid-19th century on imported soil and includes a large variety of exotic species. Several experimental areas of forest were planted, and while not perhaps commercially viable some are now managed as a recreational resource.

Water Lilies in flower

Orchids are common in summer

Many of the small lochs are covered by a carpet of Water Lilies and other aquatic plants in summer, which adds colour and interest to an otherwise rather monotonous moorland landscape.

Primroses flower in May and are particularly widespread on Barra

Butterwort is insectivorous

Remains of ancient trees are frequently found beneath the peat

Grey Seals come ashore on isolated islands in Autumn to have their pups and mate

The Western Isles are home to only a small number of indigenous mammal species. At the end of the last Ice Age there would have been no land bridge to Scotland, and thus native species are limited to Grey and Common Seals and Otters.

Grey Seals come ashore to pup and mate on many of the outlying islands, including the Monachs and Rona in Autumn, while Common Seals have their pups in early Summer. Both species can often be seen around the coast. Stornoway Harbour is a good place to see seals.

Otters are elusive, but not uncommon. They are generally seen early in the morning, or late at night along rocky shores. Ferry terminals, old piers and breakwaters are often good places to look. Spraints and tracks are much easier to see than the actual animals.

The waters around the Hebrides are home to several species of cetaceans which may often be observed from the ferry. Risso's, White-beaked and White-sided Dolphins are quite common as are Porpoises.

Whales include Minke, Killer, Pilot, and occasional Sperm and Humpbacks. Large pods of Pilot Whales are often seen offshore, while groups of young male Sperm Whales sometimes appear. Killer Whales follow the shoals of Herring in summer.

Tiumpan Head, the most easterly point on Lewis, is an excellent place from which to watch Risso's Dolphin, of which there is a resident population, and in summer, White-sided Dolphin. The water depth of over 100 metres close inshore means that Minke, Killer and other whales may occasionally be seen also.

Grey Seal pup

Otter

Risso's Dolphin are locally common

Common Seals frequent sheltered shores and sea lochs

Red Deer roam many of the hills

All cetacean watching needs patience, a sharp eye, good light and a relatively calm sea. Photography needs a very fast reaction time!

A species which may also be making a come-back is the Basking Shark, which is once again being seen regularly offshore in August and September usually.

With man came mice, ponies, deer and sheep. There are three sub-species of Field Mouse -the Hebridean, St Kildan and Barra varieties. Hares and Hedgehogs are also introductions. Voles are only present on the Uists.

Red Deer, may often be encountered on the hills, especially in the Uists and Harris. Rabbits, do much damage to crops and destabilise sand dunes, and are common, while Mink, which have escaped from farms, cause much harm to ground nesting birds, and are on the increase.

Killer Whale

Magnus Tait

Humpback Whales are occasionally seen offshore

Pilot Whales are usually in pods, which may on occasion be very large

The Standing Stones of Callanish - midsummer sunrise

Bharpa Langass chambered cairn on North Uist is well preserved

The first settlers to the Western Isles were probably Mesolithic hunter-gatherers around 7000BC, however the earliest remaining structures are the many prominent chambered cairns and a smaller number of Neolithic settlement sites.

Chambered cairns are found throughout the islands, but are particularly numerous in the Uists. Most are very ruinous, having been used as quarries over the years, or cleared out in the 19th century. Bharpa Langass on North Uist is the best-preserved, with an intact chamber, but there are many other impressive cairns to visit.

These monumental structures were used for funerary and ritual purposes and were built around 3000BC. The large scale of many suggests that society was organised and was doing quite well before it was able to spare the time and effort to create these monuments.

In contrast there is very little visible evidence of domestic settlement in the islands. Several sites have been excavated, notably Eilean Domhnuill on Loch Olabhat on North Uist, which is one of many small islets connected to the shore by a causeway. Machair sites at Udal and Northton (Harris) have yield-

ed a large amount of material and information about life in the Neolithic and have revealed substantial footings and hearths of buildings.

Pottery was found which is quite similar to that from the same period in Orkney, suggesting the existence of cultural links, as well as "ritual" carved stone objects and stone axe blades. In peaty areas the generally acidic soil conditions do not allow for the preservation of bone and other organic objects, but in the alkaline machair areas preservation is much better, especially in waterlogged conditions.

The Neolithic period was characterised by the gradual removal of the trees and scrub, which had returned after the melting of the ice, for use in construction, tools and as fuel, as well as by land clearance for agriculture. The development of peat bogs would have accelerated the loss of woodland.

Chambered cairn at Carinish, North Uist

Copies of Neolithic pots from Eilean an Taighe, N. Uist

NMS

NMS

Carved Neolithic stone object found at Balallan, East Lewis

Steinicleit, Siader, West Lewis

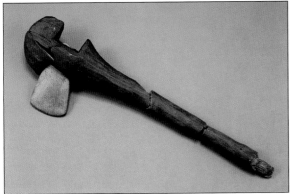

Neolithic stone-bladed axe with its carefully carved Hawthorn haft found at Shulishader on Lewis. The haft dates from about 3150BC.

Dun Bharpa, above Craigston, Barra

NEOLITHIC TIMELINE

BC	
c.11000	Ice in retreat
c.7000	First hunter-gathers arrive?
3500	Settlement at Allt Chrisal, Barra
	Unstan Ware 3150
	Carinish hearth
	Shulishader axe
	Grooved Ware
3000	Chambered Tombs
	Callanish stone ring
2500	Callanish tomb c.2000
	Chambered tombs finally sealed up

NEOLITHIC SITES TO VISIT

Lewis	Callanish
	Carn a'Mharc
	Garrabost
	Aird Dell
	Steinicleit
	Clach an Truiseil
Harris	Northton
North Uist	Bharpa Langass
	Pobull Fhinn
	Carinish
	Clettraval
	Unival
	Loch Olabhat
South Uist	Reineval
Barra	Allt Chrisal
	Dun Bharpa

ARCHAEOLOGY AND HISTORY

There are many standing stones in the Western Isles, ranging from individual monoliths to the largest and most dramatic at Callanish overlooking Loch Roag in West Lewis. Most are undated as yet, but the majority are assumed to be Neolithic monuments dating from around 3000BC.

The large stone setting at Callanish is complex with a central ring and radiating stone rows. The northern arms form an avenue which is aligned slightly east of north. Unusually there is a small chambered cairn in the centre of the ring which

post-dates the largest monolith. There are several smaller stone circles and standing stones in the area.

Various astronomical align-

ments have been suggested at Callanish, especially for sunrise and sunset at the solstices and for moonset, at the major lunar standstill which occurs every 18.6 years, when the Moon sets at its extreme northerly azimuth and the lunar eclipse cycle restarts.

Whether in fact such solar and lunar events are really part of the design of Callanish is very much open to speculation, but it is clear that the Neolithic people would have been much more acutely aware of the seasons and the regular movements of the Sun, Moon, planets and stars than modern people.

Excavations at Callanish have revealed "Grooved Ware" similar to that found in Orkney and dating from about 3000BC, as well as sherds of Beaker pottery dating from perhaps 2000BC.

There are several other smaller stone circles and

Small stone circle east of the main Callanish complex

Pobull Fhinn standing stones at Langass, North Uist

Panoramic view of the standing stones of Callanish just after dawn at midsummer

standing stones in the Callanish area, making it a must for all visiting standing stones enthusiasts.

The smaller stone circle at Pobull Fhinn in North Uist is also very dramatic and commands a panoramic view over Loch Eport, the North and South Lees and Eaval to the east, and the flat expanse of North Uist to the south.

The majority of the other monoliths throughout the islands seem to be isolated, but some as at Gramsdale on Benbecula are the remnants of circles, or are near to chambered cairns. The original function of such large standing stones as Clach an Truiseil on Lewis, or Clach Mor a'Che on North Uist is not clear but there are legends about each one.

Clach Mor a'Che, North Uist

Gramsdale Stones, Benbecula - only one monolith remains upright

STANDING STONES TO VISIT	
Lewis	Callanish
	below Steinicleit
	Clach an Truiseil
	Achmore
Gt Bernera	above bridge
Harris	Traigh Iar
North Uist	Pobull Fhinn
	Somach Coir'Fhinn
	Clach Mor a'Che
	Carinish
Benbecula	Gramsdale
South Uist	above Stoneybridge
	Pollochar
Barra	Borve machair

Replica Iron Age house at Bosta, Great Bernera

The "Atlantic Roundhouse" is often used to describe the series of domestic building styles prevalent in western and northern scotland from about 700BC to early medieval times. The lack of timber meant that stone was used for the walls and they were often built on small islands on lochs or on small hills.

It now seems that roundhouses, duns and brochs are all part of an evolution in building styles. All of the duns so far excavated have intra-mural cells, galleries or stairs resembling the larger brochs. Good examples are scattered throughout the islands from Loch an Duna in Lewis to Barra Head lighthouse.

The most prominent and best-preserved broch is Dun Carloway, not far from Callanish. It is built on a rocky hillock, in common with many other more ruinous such monuments.

As in all brochs, the walls are hollow, and bound together with large lintels, which also form the floors of the galleries and the stairs. The walls are over 3m thick at the base, and while the interior walls rise vertically from the scarcement at about 2m from the floor, the exterior walls slope in considerably. The maximum height is about 9m.

Brochs and duns in the Western Isles seem to have been isolated structures, and not usually surrounded by settlements as in Orkney. While those situated on islets on lochs would have had easy access to water, those on rocky knolls would not.

Excavation has shown that these houses were really farmhouses, often with long occupation histories, rather than strongholds, and perhaps more a product of fashion rather than defence needs. The broch towers had more than one internal wooden floor, which were accessed by the internal stairway.

Broch near Traigh na Berie, Lewis

Well-preserved broch - Dun Torcuill, North Uist

The smaller duns would not have had more than one level and indeed the blackhouses which persisted into the 19th century would not have been that much different inside.

A replica Pictish era house at Bosta in Great Bernera gives a good insight into how spacious such buildings were, and provides an interesting contrast to the nearby actual ruined houses.

Another development was the wheelhouse, which was built on the machair but also inland, by first digging a large hole, and then lining it with a stone wall. Further stone walls were then built radially to support the exterior walls from collapsing inwards and the structure roofed over. Unfortunately the only well-preserved such houses are in Jarlshof in Shetland.

There are a number of promontory forts in the Western Isles also. The best examples are at *Rubha na Beirgh* near the Butt of Lewis, *Caisteal Odair* on the north-west point of North Uist, and near the lighthouse on Barra Head.

Wheelhouse at Allt Chrisal, overlooking Vatersay Sound, Barra

Interior stairway, Dun Carloway

Remote broch at Dun an Ruadh, Pabbay

BRONZE & IRON AGES TIMELINE

BC	
c.2000	Bronze Age
	Beakers first appear
1500	Peat bogs developing
c.800	Callanish abandoned
700	Iron Age round houses
600	Oldest Broch deposits
100	Brochs at peak
100AD	Brochs abandoned

BRONZE AND IRON AGE SITES TO VISIT

Lewis	Callanish
	Dun Carloway
	Riff
	Loch a Dun
Gt Bernera	Dun Bharabhat
	Houses, Bosta
Harris	Northton
North Uist	Clettraval
	Dun Torcuill
	Dun Sticir
Benbecula	Dun Buidhe
South Uist	Loch a Bharp
	Dun Mor
	Dun Uiselan
	Kilphedar Aisled House
Barra	Allt Chrisal wheelhouse
	Dun Scurrival
	Dun Ban
	Pabbay
	Barra Head

ARCHAEOLOGY AND HISTORY

One of the "Lewis Chessmen" found at Uig Bay in 1831

The Vikings were already settling in Orkney by the late 8th century, and first attacked Iona in 795AD. They must therefore already have been familiar with the Western Isles by that time, and Norse domination of the western seaboard of Scotland was to continue for over 450 years.

They were variously referred to as *Lochlannaich* - Fjordmen, *Finngaills* - White Foreigners, *Nordmanni* - Northmen, or simply *Vikinir*. During this time the Western Isles were often referred to as the *Innse Gall* - Islands of Foreigners - by the Scots and Irish, and as the *Sudreyar* - Southern Isles - by the Vikings themselves.

Although few written records exist from this time apart from a few saga mentions, there is much place-name and linguistic evidence for the Norse settlement, especially in Lewis where a large proportion of townships and natural features have names of Norse derivation. Western Isles Gaelic also incorporates many words of Norse derivation.

Although probably nominally Pictish at the time of the first Viking incursions only a few symbol and cross inscribed stones and distinctive houses have been found in the Western Isles, suggesting communication with Mainland Pictish culture was limited. However the existence of several Pabbays, implies that Celtic monks were present when the Norsemen arrived.

Very few distinctively Norse artefacts have been found, apart from several pagan burials at Cnip on Lewis and on Hirta. Indeed the richest find was the 12th century "Lewis Chessmen" found in 1831 at Uig Bay. The Norse influence in the west stretched from Lewis to the Isle of Man and settlement towns in Ireland. In addition sagas tell us that the first immigrants to Iceland

Viking grave being excavated at Traigh na Berie, West Lewis

were from the Hebrides, no doubt of Norse-Gaelic descent, who left to avoid paying Norwegian taxes. It now seems that the Norse settlement may have been relatively peaceful, unlike the Viking raids.

A most interesting Celtic/Norse inscribed stone was found at Cille Bharra, on Barra. This stone has both Christian Celtic and Runic Norse symbols.

The island site now occupied by Kisimul Castle is said to have been the site of 11th century Viking fortifications, and it seems likely that something similar may have existed at Stornoway with its excellent harbour.

Several Norse domestic sites have been excavated, at Barvas in Lewis, Udal in North Uist as well as Drimore and Kildonan in South Uist, but no Norse era building is able to be viewed by the public. No doubt most have been built over by succeeding generations.

During the early Norse period the Western Isles were used as Viking bases, and were at various times under the nominal control of the Earl of Orkney or the King of Man, under the King of Norway.

Two Norse silver hoards have been discovered in the Western Isles including at Oronsay, North Uist (c.1780) and in the Castle Grounds, Stornoway in 1988.

NMS

Viking gilt bronze brooches and necklace found at Cnip, Lewis

Kisimul Castle, Castlebay, Barra

Celtic/Norse stone from Barra

VIKING AGE TIMELINE

AD	
c.500	Irish "papae" arriving
795	Iona first attacked
995	Sigurd the Strong baptised by force
c.1000	Sigurd makes Earl Gilli Governor
1014	Battle of Clontarf, Isles under Kingdom of Man
1066	Stamford Bridge
1098	King Magnus Barelegs' expedition
1156	Loss of Southern Hebrides
1263	"Battle" of Largs
1266	Treaty of Perth

SITES TO VISIT

Lewis	Uig Sands
	Lews Castle grounds
	Cnip
	Stornoway
	St Olav's Church
Harris	Northton
North Uist	Udal
South Uist	Drimore
	Kildonan
	Calvay Island
Barra	Kisimul Castle
	Cille Bharra
St Kilda	Village Bay

ARCHAEOLOGY AND HISTORY

Replica Birlinn "Aileach" which sailed from Ireland to the Faeroes - this development of the Viking longship was fast, seaworthy and easy to handle.

During the 9th century, when the kingdoms of Dalriada and Pictland merged under Kenneth MacAlpin, the centre of power of the new Kingdom of Scotland moved eastward, while Norse power was increasing on the western seaboard. The title **"Lord of the Isles"** originates from the 10th century when Norse rulers, who depended on the sea to wield power, were referred to in Gaelic as *Ri Innse Gall* - King of the Isles of Foreigners (Norsemen). Around 1100 the western Mainland came under Scottish control, while the Isles remained under Norway and were controlled by Scottish-Norse families.

In about 1156 the Norse-Scottish **Somerled**, married to the granddaughter of the first *Ri Innse Gall* (Godfrey of the Isle of Man), took control of the Southern Hebrides. Chieftains in the Hebrides had always had divided loyalties until 1266, when the **Treaty of Perth** handed the Hebrides to Scotland. Prior to this the Hebrides were controlled by a mix of the

Norwegian Crown, the Kings of Man, the Earls of Orkney, and various Irish Kings. Norse power in the west was waning in the later 13th century while the Scots were becoming more interested in the islands, and after the unsuccessful campaign of the Norse King Haakon Haakonson in 1263, allegiance was to the Scottish Crown although Scotland still had to pay an annual rent to Norway until 1468, when Orkney was impignorated to Scotland.

However the principal families remained fiercely independent, taking sides in the Wars of Independence, where some gained much and others lost everything. In particular Angus Og MacDonald's support for Robert the Bruce gained him much power and influence, and enabled him to greatly increase his family's interests in the Hebrides.

In 1354 John of Islay, son of Angus Og, took on the title of *Dominus Insularum*, having supported David II and then

Robert Stewart (later Robert II), and achieved more control of the Hebrides than anyone before him. He died in 1387 when he ruled the Hebrides from Islay to Lewis and large areas of the adjacent Mainland, but not Skye. This power was centred on Islay and depended on having control of the sea. His successors strove to expand their power until eventually John of Islay plotted with Edward IV of England against the Scottish Crown. This was a step too far and his title was forfeited in 1475, and finally again in 1493.

Despite attempts to regain the title by various MacDonalds, the existence of such a centre of power within Scotland was too big a threat to the Kingdom to be allowed to revive. Today the Prince of Wales holds the honorary title of "Lord of the Isles".

The West Highland Galley,

Birlinn carving at Rodel Church

Dun MacLeoid, Barra

(ON *Byrdingr* - cargo ship), or **Birlinn**, which was the basis of all power in the Hebrides and West Highlands, developed from the Viking longship. In the 12ᵗʰ century the starboard rudders started to be replaced with stern-hung rudders. These open boats had sails and oars for propulsion and were very well suited to the waters of the area whether for military, piracy, trade or fishing uses.

Sea transport was vital to the Hebrides as elsewhere in Britain, and the Birlinn was a development of the Viking longship, smaller and more manouverable. These fast and seaworthy vessels enabled the Lords of the Isles and their successors easy means of transport around the isles for lawful and less lawful activities. Similar craft

Weaver's Castle off Eriskay is said to have been a pirate's stronghold

remained in use until the end of the 19ᵗʰ century.

By the start of the 17ᵗʰ century the government had started to take strong measures against the owners of Birlinns, particularly after the Union of the Crowns in 1603, when transport of Hebridean mercenaries to Ireland came to an end. After this large boats were superseded by smaller versions suited to inshore fishing and communication between islands rather than

carrying large crews of fighting men and their booty.

In 1991 a replica galley called the *Aileach* sailed up the west coast of Scotland and on to the Faeroes. This boat was built in the west of Ireland in a manner very similar to Viking ships. Many small fishing boats around the Hebrides are still clinker built, but sadly wood construction has almost universally given way to fibre glass.

Iron Age broch, Dun Sticir, on North Uist, was reused in Medieval times

Borve Castle on Benbecula is said to have been a stronghold of Clanranald

LORDS OF THE ISLES TIMELINE

AD	
1098	King Magnus Barelegs' expedition
1156	Somerled takes Southern Hebrides
1263	"Battle" of Largs
1266	Treaty of Perth
1354	John of Islay - "Lord of the Isles"
1493	Lordship of the Isles forfeit
1603	Union of the Crowns

SITES TO VISIT

Lewis	Stornoway
	Dun Eistean, Ness
Harris	Rodel Church
North Uist	Dun Sticir
	Teampall na Trionaid
Benbecula	Borve Castle
South Uist	Weaver's Castle
	Caisteal Beagram
	Calvay Castle
Barra	Kisimul Castle
	Dun MacLeoid

St Ronan's Chapel on Rona may date from as early as the 7ᵗʰ century.

There are many ancient chapel sites in the Western Isles, and while there is no evidence that St Columba ever visited any of the Isles, the people must have felt the influence of the Irish seaborne monks from the late 6ᵗʰ century onwards. Place-name evidence suggests that *Papar* - priests were present at the time the Vikings arrived, and there are several Pabbays (ON *Papa-oy* - Priest's Island) in the area. Incised stones with crosses have been found at several locations, and there are dedications to several Irish saints.

The two oldest extant chapels are on remote islands. On Rona *(Ronaidh)* where the chapel may date from the late 7ᵗʰ or early 8ᵗʰ century there is a small *"oratory"* or cell with corbelled roof at its east end. The church is surrounded by an oval enclosure with many cross-shaped grave markers, some of which may be 7ᵗʰ to 9ᵗʰ century and others 12ᵗʰ or 13ᵗʰ. The dedication may or may not be to the real St Ronan as the name Rona may be Norse (ON *Hraun-oy* - rough island).

On Sula Sgeir there are several beehive cells with corbelled roofs. St Ronan's sister is said to have gone there where she was later found dead with a shag nesting in her chest cavity. St Flann's Chapel on *Eilean Mhor* in the Flannan Isles is another small stone-built chapel of Irish type on an inaccessible island.

Cille Bharra on Barra is dedicated to St Barr, or Finbar. There are three chapels on the site, which may date from Norse times. An interesting carved stone was found in 1865 with runes on one side and a Celtic cross on the other, which is from the 10ᵗʰ or 11ᵗʰ century. There are also three medieval tombstones which may have been grave markers from MacNeill chiefs of Barra.

At Howmore on South Uist there are ruins of several medieval chapels. The largest, of which only the east gable remains, is *Teampall Mor*, which may date from the 13ᵗʰ century, while the other three chapels are smaller and newer. The site is the burial place of the chiefs of Clan Ranald.

Teampall na Trionaid at

The chapels at Howmore may date from the 13ᵗʰ century

Teampall Mholuaidh at Eoropie, Ness, Lewis

Carinish in North Uist is said to have been founded by Beahag, daughter of Somerled in the 12th century. It was a school in the middle ages and is mentioned in 14th century records. Today the buildings are ruinous but in the 19th century the church was said to have had carved stone decoration and a spire.

The old church dedicated to St Columba at Aignish may date from the 14th century. There is a gravestone to Margaret, daughter of Ruairi, who was chief of the MacLeods of Lewis and who died in 1503. The surrounding ancient cemetery is being eroded by the sea.

Teampall Mholuaidh at Ness is dedicated to the Irish St Moluag. It may date from the 16th century or earlier and is the site of an ancient cult where the sea-god Shony was celebrated on All Saints Day. The church was renovated in the early 20th century.

On Benbecula there is an ancient chapel at Nunton which is dedicated to the Virgin Mary and associated with a nunnery, whose stones were used to build Clanranald's house and steading in the 18th century. The convent may also have had connections with the Monach Islands. *Teampall Chaluim Cille* is now just a ruin on small mound near Balivanich, but gave the village its name, *Baile na Mhanaich* - Township of the Monks and is said to have been established by St Torranan from Ireland, who landed at Calligeo - the Geo of the Monks. Apparently this monastery continued to function until the 17th century.

The church at Rodel in Harris is dedicated to St Clement and is the second largest medieval church in the Hebrides. It was built in the 1520's by MacLeod of Dunvegan whose grandiose tomb occupies the south west wall of the choir. By the 18th century the church was disused, but it was renovated in the 18th and 19th centuries. The tower has several interesting carved stone ornaments. Alexander MacLeod's tomb dominates the east end of the church and there are several other interesting gravestones in the north transept. There is a good view of the Sound of Harris from the tower.

Grave at Aignish Church (Eaglais na h-Aoidhe)

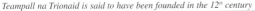

Teampall na Trionaid is said to have been founded in the 12th century

A crofting couple at work outside their blackhouse

clan did not actually "own" the land, although under the feudal system it was nevertheless held under the overlordship of the King. In the wake of the civil war new laws made the chiefs proprietors - in modern language the land was nationalised at zero compensation and given to the clan chiefs for nothing. These chiefs of course proceeded to live and act in the manner of landed gentry elsewhere, but had to find a means to generate the income to keep them in their new-found status.

The present system of land tenure in the Western Isles is the result of local, national and international events over the last 250 years. Up until the 1745-46 Jacobite rebellion and its violent aftermath the West Highlands and Islands of Scotland were pretty much left to themselves by successive Scottish and then British governments. However the aftermath of Culloden with its brutal repression of the ancient clan system, which had survived in the area long after such systems had died out elsewhere, was to result in centuries of hardship, destitution, emigration for the people and depredation of the landscape. The results are still very evident today.

Until 1745 most of the land in the Highlands and Islands was held under a system whereby the clan controlled ownership. The chief of the

The system of land tenure was most likely little changed since prehistoric times and was essentially a community-based society of subsistence farming, augmented with a little inshore fishing. The society was based around the clan system whereby the chief could demand men to bear arms in times of emergency but otherwise the people got leave to get on with life. Hebridean Galleys were a major source of power and influence in a time when inter-clan and inter-family conflict was common. This type of society was outmoded by the 18th century and change was inevitable, violent or otherwise.

During the French Wars many products and raw materials were in short supply and either prices became elevated or alternatives were sought. Small black cattle

Children outside their blackhouse home

had long been a sought after product of the Highlands and Islands and their prices soared. At the same time the ready supplies of seaweed provided the ideal raw material to make kelp, a good source of potash for glass making and munitions, then in short supply.

Kelp is made by burning dried seaweed in pits. The process is very labour-intensive, but given a ready supply of cheap labour it could be very productive for the land "owner". At the same time sheep farming was becoming very attractive with high prices both for mutton and wool due to the booming industrial revolution in the south.

Accordingly small tenants were cleared off the land upon which they had lived for centuries and forcibly relocated in areas suitable for kelp-making on plots of land too small to be viable on their own.

Inevitably with the cessation of hostilities the "kelp boom" came to an end and suddenly the "proprietors" had no further need for the large population of small tenants. This was aggravated by famine in the late 1840's due to potato blight and bad harvests. Despite some famine relief effort the government and land "owners" invoked a major emigration programme to Canada and Australia which

Burning seaweed on the shore to make kelp - back-breaking work

was to result in the loss of tens of thousands of people from the Highlands and Islands - much to the ultimate benefit of their destination countries.

Lazy beds on fertile Jurassic rock at Airighean a'Baigh, Shiant Islands

The contrasting grandeur of Clanranald's mansion at Ormiclate, South Uist

Memorial to the "Pairc Land Raid" - part of the "Land Wars"

During the late 18th and 19th centuries the Established Church ministers usually tended to err on the side of landowners and sheep farmers and did not often support tenants or criticise evictions. There was a growth of religious revival and evangelism which was greatly aided by the publication of the Gaelic Bible and church schools.

In 1843 the Disruption and establishment of the Free Church of Scotland was seen as a victory for the crofters but as a threat by the landowners, and

Great Bernera cairn

was one of the seeds from which grew the surge of opposition to landlordism by the crofters and their supporters.

The history of land-holding in the Western Isles is quite different to Orkney and Shetland, which remained Norse until 1468, and where the land was held under Udal law. Under this system much of the land was held under owner-occupation, ever since the first Norse settlement in the 9th century, while the rest was held by the earl, church or king. Udalers owned their land absolutely and could not be "cleared" nearly so easily. Also the Norse dominance in the north was complete, whereas this may never have been the case in the west.

The lack of leases and security of tenure for crofters meant that there was no incentive to improve houses, buildings or agricultural practices and an indifference to stock breeding,

resulting in poor quality animals and low cattle prices. During the 1880's wool prices crashed and many sheep farms were turned over to deer forests. At the same time the crofters finally started to take action themselves and from 1881 until the 1920's there were a series of rent strikes, land seizures, and refusals to obey courts and officials.

Throughout the Western Isles "lazybeds" or *feannagan* may be seen, often on the most inhospitable of places. These ridges were raised by people evicted from their homes and forced to glean a living elsewhere. The lazybeds were created from anything but laziness, and involved carting seaweed, plus animal manure and domestic midden to the area to augment the meagre turf which was present to grow potatoes and grain.

The "Land Wars" are now commemorated by a series of cairns which have been erected on Great Bernera, at Gress, Aignish and Pairc on Lewis. The actions of these crofters in the 1880's were to be the catalyst for change in the control of crofting lands, but the outcome did not immediately solve all of their problems.

Public opinion in the country was changing in favour of the crofters, due to very successful political campaigning. The Napier Commission on crofting was set up in 1883 and reported in 1884, and the Crofters Act of 1886 finally gave crofters security of tenure and compensation for buildings and improvements as well as power to fix rents. However the Act did not solve the other central problems for crofters and cottars which were the severe lack of land and the issue of land ownership.

In 1897 the Government finally started to purchase more land for crofters and it was after the First World War before the Board of Agriculture finally seriously addressed the issue by eventually purchasing over 200,000 acres of land for crofts.

During the 20th century there have been many attempts to solve the "Highland Problem", however the central issue of land ownership remains. Apart from ensuring the continued fossiliza-tion of "traditional" crofting (in fact a creation of the early 19th century), the fact that the people mostly remain as tenants who do not own or control the land combined with the system of government grants to crofters is probably the single factor which most limits economic development in the islands.

The result is that most young people do not return home to work after their education, and depopulation is a serious threat for many of the remoter areas. Only a fundamental reform of land tenure where local communities have much more influence on land usage can begin to allow the potential for social and economic progression and thus viable local populations. With the new Acts which are due to come into force in 2002 it is to be hoped that at least a part of the land ownership problem will finally be solved.

The Stornoway area was for long unique in that the land belongs to the Stornoway Trust which administers it on behalf of the people, the only area to accept Lord Leverhulme's offer of ownership in 1923. Recently the Valtos Estate in West Lewis was also acquired by the crofters, and it is likely that further such developments may take place, as has happened elsewhere such as on the islands of Eigg and Gigha in the Inner Hebrides.

Aignish cairn (above)   *Gress Cairn (below)*

"LAND WARS" TIMELINE

c.1760	Sheep farming
c.1800	Crofting system introduced
1843	The Disruption in the Kirk
1850's	Many evictions
1874	Bernera Riot
1884	Napier Commission
1886	Crofters Act
1888	Aignish Riot
1919	Coll and Gress raids
1923	Stornoway Trust

SITES TO VISIT

Lewis	Stornoway
	Arnol blackhouse
	Gress
	Aignish
	Great Bernera
	Pairc
	Uig
Harris	Leverburgh
	"Golden Road"
North Uist	Lochmaddy
	Sollas
Benbecula	Nunton
South Uist	Eriskay
Barra	Vatersay
	Castlebay

History and Culture

Girl herding sheep at Ness, Lewis

Crofting remains an important part of the social and economic life of the Western Isles. There are over 6,000 crofts, but few are large enough to provide a living. Although crofters have had the right to buy their land for the price of a few years' rent few have opted for this due to the way in which agricultural support grants apply to crofting.

Most crofters have other jobs, or are retired. There are also a few small farms, especially on the Uists. The main production is Blackface lambs for fattening on the Scottish Mainland. Cattle are also kept on the Uists and Barra, where grazing is better, and holdings bigger. Hay, silage and some oats are grown for winter fodder as well as potatoes for home use.

By its nature crofting is a low-intensity method of agriculture and as such is environmentally friendly. Most crofters have one or more additional occupation, traditionally weaving or fishing, but now just as likely to be in a Stornoway office or on an oil rig, but the land has helped to retain the scattered rural population structure.

Young people have always left the Western Isles for further education and work. In the past many men joined the Royal or Merchant Navy, or worked on fishing boats, while their wives and children looked after the croft. This is still the case today, as many emigrate to the Mainland or abroad to find work, with the result that in several parts of the islands the population is in severe decline.

There will be a new Land Reform Act in 2002 which among other things extends the rights of crofters to buy their land and legislates on rights of access for the public. Whether such reforms will do anything to assist progress in the Western Isles remains to be seen.

Taking in the peat - there are lots of "Old Fergies" about

Highland cow on Harris

34

At present sheep and wool prices are very low, and only the subsidies paid by the Government make rearing sheep viable at all. Cattle prices are more buoyant, but the market today is for larger, faster growing breeds, which are inherently unsuited to the small scale environment of crofting. Some crofters keep Highland Cattle, or Highland crosses, which are hardy enough to outwinter and meet a speciality beef market.

The crofting community has always believed that the land was theirs. It was only with the changes which took place after 1745 when clan chiefs became "proprietors" - "landowners" in need of cash to support their life styles - and the old system of clan allegiance was broken, that the present system of landholding developed. It is to be hoped that the early 21st century will see the process of reform continued to the ultimate benefit of the local communities.

Peat bank on North Uist - much peat is still cut by crofters for winter fuel

Herding sheep on Barra

Potatoes grow very well in the sandy machair soil

Crofter with sheep, South Uist

Cultivating the machair, South Uist

Interior of No 42 Arnol, West Lewis

The roof was then covered with slatted planks supported by purlins. A layer of heather turf was put in place and finally the roof was thatched with oat or bere straw, or Marram Grass, and tied down with heather ropes weighted with stones.

Drains were incorporated to remove rainwater and effluent from the byre end which was at the lower end of the house. Often a small barn was attached to one side. The "ben" end was often just one room, but in later houses, as at Arnol, there was a living room/kitchen and a sleeping room with box beds. A cooking pot or kettle was suspended over an open peat fire in the middle of the floor. Many blackhouses were later modified to have chimneys and hearths and became "whitehouses" of which there are many examples in the Uists.

The preserved and reconstructed blackhouse at 42, Arnol in Lewis was inhabited until 1965, having been built in 1885. It is one of the last remaining examples of a long tradition of house-building which goes back to Viking times or earlier where people and domestic animals shared the same subrectangular buildings. Blackhouses are so-named because they had no chimneys, the smoke escaping through the thatched roof.

The name also had a derogatory connotation which implied that the inhabitants were not very civilised - an assumption which was based on no evidence as many eminent master mariners, doctors, engineers and other educated people originated in such places throughout the Highlands and Islands.

Where wood was available such houses were usually built from stone and turf on a stone foundation with wooden lining. Many ruins of these houses may be seen all over the Western Isles, where they were built of stone, no doubt due to the lack of wood. The walls are double-skinned with a filling of clay and small stones between the inner and outer faces and up to 2m thick, while the roofs were formed from driftwood or whalebone couples which rested on the inner wall.

The peat reek acted as a disinfectant and deodorant, and the sooty thatch made good manure. The proximity of people and cattle perhaps reduced tuberculosis to some extent as the ammonia from the cattle urine is known to kill the bacillus - dairy maids rarely contracted the disease.

Heather rope and Willow baskets

Box beds at "ben" end of house

Blackhouses may appear primitive but they were well-adapted to the climate and resources available to their inhabitants. The traditional breed of black cattle was small and easily handled and would have provided milk, cheese and butter. Some sheep, a pig and hens would have been kept while fish would have added to the staple diet of potatoes. Fish and meat would have been smoked in the rafters, or salted down for winter. The houses may have been unhygenic by our standards, but they would have been cosy in winter gales, and could be built out of local materials by the community at almost no cost in terms of money.

Across the road from 42 Arnol, a more recent 20th century house has been preserved as an example of the type of dwelling which replaced blackhouses. It is a two-up two-down house typical of many in rural Scotland and is furnished in the manner of the 1950's, with many interesting artefacts from the time. The small shop and visitor centre next door sells admission tickets and souvenirs.

Thatched cottage with chimneys and lazy beds, Howmore, South Uist

Norse-type mill and barn, Shawbost, West Lewis

Thatched house with extension and chimneys, Ardheisker, North Uist

Interior of early 20th century house showing box bed

Range and furniture in early 20th century house

Spinning wool by hand, Procropool, Harris

People have made woven woollen cloth for a very long time, and the traditional Hebridean Sheep was bred for weaving rather than for knitting as in Shetland. The wool is strong and makes a tough thread ideal for weaving, which results in a hard-wearing textile. Traditionally it was the women who did the spinning, weaving and waulking and there are many customs and songs relating to the various processes.

Originally everything was done by hand which limited output and thus the quantity available for sale or barter.

In the past the wool was dyed using various plants such as *Crotal* (lichen) - browns, Lady's Bedstraw - reds, Alder - black, Heather - green and Birch - yellow. The wool was boiled up outside in a large iron pot until the required colour was obtained. Obtaining fast and beautiful colours from local plants was a major part of the skill involved producing tweed. Once woven the cloth had to be laboriously "waulked" by hand. After soaking in urine the cloth was laid out on a table and thumped back and fore by a group of women, who sang special waulking songs during the process which shrank the cloth and gave it more body and strength - a process akin to felting.

In 1842 the dowager Countess of Dunmore, who owned much of Harris, became interested and soon "Harris Tweed" was popular with sportsmen all over the country. By the late 19th century demand was greater than supply and gradually dyeing, carding, spinning and finishing became mechanised. All weaving was (and still is) done by hand by crofters at home. In 1909 a trade mark of the Harris Tweed Association was registered by the Harris Tweed Association (now Authority) which controls quality and production methods.

The introduction of the "Hattersley" loom in the 1920's, though still human powered, allowed much more efficient production and a greater range of designs and cloth weights.

Weaving on a traditional wooden loom, Procropool, Harris

Tweed awaiting despatch

Harris Tweed Authority

Although the industry has declined somewhat in recent years the clicking of looms in small sheds is a frequent sound in the Western Isles and it remains a substantial part of the local economy. The traditional width of the cloth is 30 inches, but many weavers are now using new double width looms.

Weaver at work on his Hattersley loom, West Lewis

The 1993 Harris Tweed Act states that the tweed *"must be hand-woven by islanders at their homes in the Outer Hebrides and made from pure virgin wool dyed and spun in the Outer Hebrides"*. Marketing of the cloth is done by the HTA and by the main mills, the biggest of which is Kenneth MacKenzie Ltd.

Harris Tweed is sold all around the world, but the vagaries of fashion and ups and downs of economies, mean that demand fluctuates.The "orb" trade mark symbol is the customers guarantee of genuine quality in a product *"created for individuals by individuals"*.

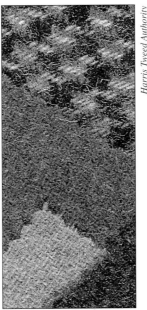

Samples of Harris Tweed

Harris Tweed

HAND WOVEN IN THE OUTER HEBRIDES

"Orb symbol" Trade Mark

Rolls of finished Harris Tweed

Hattersley loom

OIFIC A' PHUIST
BAGH A' CHAISTEIL

Post Office sign - Castlebay

Today the majority of the population of the Western Isles understand Gaelic, and for many it is the language of everyday life, despite the onslaught of English. It is not clear what language the inhabitants spoke before the arrival of the Vikings, but presumably it was similar to other parts of the north and west of Scotland. A large proportion of the place names in the Isles are directly Old Norse (ON), while many more are Gaelic (G) translations from Old Norse.

Hebridean Gaelic has numerous loanwords from Old Norse, but what is perhaps surprising is the lack of influence over grammar despite Viking control lasting for nearly 500 years. The language has also picked up many English and Latin loanwords, but of course English has also many Gaelic words. It was to be the 19th century before the combination of the Church and the Gaelic Bible taught many people to read and write their language, while at the same time the introduction of school education for all was at first in English, although this was subsequently relaxed.

Today official attitudes to Gaelic are much more positive than in the past. The political need to destroy the clan system after 1745, plus increasing need to travel to find work, ensured that many Hebrideans had to learn English, just as did the many emigrants. Gaelic culture in all its forms now receives a large amount of public support for radio, TV and publications, as well as music and other arts and education. There are worries that many young people do not use the language as much as they might, but this is perhaps understandable when so many have to leave to find education and work.

To the visitor Hebridean culture seems alive and well. People from the Western Isles have always travelled far and wide to work, there are also many new residents who have come from other parts of UK who take part in Gaelic culture. The mix of old and new, languages, people, and impending reform especially in land-holding after the continual changes in local society over the last 250 years are in many ways good for the culture. After the tribulations of the 19th and early 20th centuries the prospects for the Western Isles seem very positive.

The Christian religion remains central to the life of the community in the Western Isles and the Sabbath is strictly observed on Lewis and Harris as well as North Uist where the people are mostly Presbyterians of the Free Church of Scotland. There are no ferries, flights or shops open, although most hotels serve meals to visitors. In Barra

Arnol Blackhouse signpost

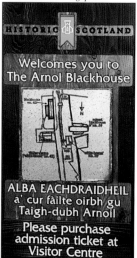

HISTORIC SCOTLAND

Welcomes you to
The Arnol Blackhouse

ALBA EACHDRAIDHEIL
a' cur fàilte oirbh gu
Taigh-dubh Arnol

Please purchase
admission ticket at
Visitor Centre

and South Uist the Roman Catholic faith predominates and Sundays are observed in a more relaxed manner. Wherever they are, visitors wishing to attend church should first ascertain in which language the service will be in, as many are in Gaelic.

There are many Gaelic cultural events which take place during the year, including, the Hebridean Celtic Festival in Lewis, Ceolas Music Summer School in South Uist, Harris Arts Festival and Barra Live. Several **Mods** - with traditional singing, piping, dancing, music, poetry, story telling and drama - also take place during the year.

There are annual sporting events, Highland Games, regattas, annual galas or festivals and agricultural shows in several places throughout the isles.

19th century church interior, Hirta, St Kilda

19th century school classroom, Hirta, St Kilda

Bagh a Chaisteil (Taobh an Iar) 》

《 Bagh a Chaisteil (Taobh an Ear)

Signs to Castlebay, Barra - west side and east side

Gaelic/English road signs on Lewis

Shrine on Eriskay- typical of the Southern Isles

Dalbeg beach, West Lewis

Isle of Lewis - *Eilean Leodhais*

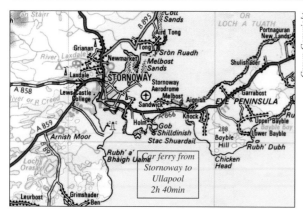

STORNOWAY - *Steornabhagh* (ON *Stjornavagr* - Steering or Anchorage Bay) is one of the best natural harbours in the Hebrides and by far the largest settlement in the Western Isles (population about 8,000). The original settlement was probably in the vicinity of Point Street, but no buildings remain which are older than late 18th century.

Herring fishing drew the Dutch, English and Lowland Scots to the area in the 17th century and the town developed into a major fishing port during the 19th century. Most of the main buildings date from this time or later, and the oldest is said to be the 18th or early 19th century **Fishermen's Coop** building on North Beach.

The medieval **Castle** was the stronghold of the MacLeods who were said to be descended from the 12th century Norseman, Olav the Black, King of Man and the Isles. It is highly likely that there was a Viking stronghold on this site, and perhaps an Iron Age broch before that, although there is no evidence.

MacLeods dominated Lewis for about 400 years. The castle was the scene of dramatic events on several occasions. In 1506 Crown troops under the Earl of Huntly besieged it whilst searching for the forfeited Donald *Dubh* MacDonald - Lord of the Isles. It was finally destroyed in 1654 by Cromwell's soldiers and the remains are under the old ro-ro pier.

In 1598 James VI declared Lewis forfeit to the MacLeods and he granted the island to the "Fife Adventurers" who were to

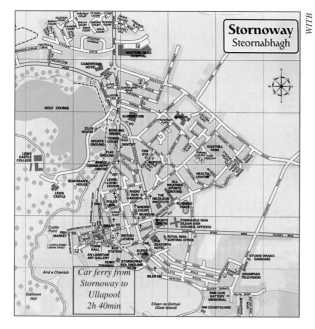

Stornoway from Lews Castle

civilise and colonise it. In October 1598 they arrived at Stornoway along with 600 soldiers. However much the settlers may have achieved they were chased off the island and their houses burned. The MacLeods were temporarily in charge again, but in 1607 ownership again passed to the remaining settlers.

By 1610 the MacKenzie Earl of Seaforth was in control and the family was to remain so until 1844. In 1628 Stornoway became a Royal Burgh, but only for a short time due to objections from other towns. The excellent harbour and rich fishing grounds of the Minch have ensured that fish has always been important to the town. Today whitefish and shellfish are the most important fisheries, and the Herring and Mackerel are landed elsewhere.

In 1653 Cromwell's army built a fort in the town. By 1695 there were about 60 families in Stornoway and a church and school, while by 1796 the population was 2,639. Herring was the main source of wealth to the town, which was a major fishing

port for over 200 years.

After the purchase of Lewis in 1844 by James Matheson considerable development took place in the town and Lews Castle was built - all financed from the selling of opium in

China. The Castle is now owned by the Council, but is very much in need of renovation. Behind it the modern buildings of Lews College, a part of the University of the Highlands and Islands, reflects a newer philosophy.

The Fishermen's Coop building on North Beach is one of the oldest buildings

Fishing Boats in the harbour

Lews Castle from North Beach

South Beach, Stornoway from the old ferry pier

Stornoway Golf Course is in the Castle grounds on the edge of town

Arnish Point Lighthouse, which was first lit in 1852

There is a panoramic view of Stornoway from the top of Gallows Hill. This area was planted by the Mathesons and is especially attractive during Spring and Summer, with over 70 species of trees and shrubs and many wild flowers - in strong contrast to the rest of the mostly treeless islands.

An old sawmill near the Castle has recently been renovated by the Stornoway Trust, creating the **Woodland Centre**, which has an excellent cafeteria, small shop and interpretative displays about the Castle grounds, which are being greatly improved. There are several interesting waymarked walks to follow. The **Golf Course** is also nearby.

Lord Leverhulme of Unilever bought the island in 1918. He had grandiose ideas about developing Stornoway as an industrial fishing port, but despite investing large sums he failed to get the support of the crofters of Lewis. He then offered ownership of all of Lewis to the people but only Stornoway accepted. Title to the town and parish of Stornoway was transferred to the Town Council in 1923. It is now administered by the **Stornoway Trust** which until recently was unique as a form of community land ownership.

The harbour is always interesting and is base to a large number of small fishing boats. Most fish for prawns, scallops or whitefish in the Minch. The harbour fills up with the colourful fleet on Saturday nights as crews spend Sunday ashore. Catches are

Stornoway War Memorial

Stornoway in the 1820's by William Daniel - with the ruined castle

landed at the fish market here, or at Kinlochbervie, Ullapool or Mallaig.

An Lanntair Arts Centre is currently in the Old Town Hall, but will move into new purpose-built premises opposite the ferry terminal when construction is complete. There are regular exhibitions of work by local, national, and international artists, while the coffee shop has excellent views over the harbour. The shop stocks an interesting range of books, cards and quality crafts.

The **Lewis Loom Centre** in the Old Grainstore at 3 Bayhead should not be missed. The tour includes explanations of the structure of different wools, dyeing, spinning and weaving and there are some unusual things for sale in the little shop.

Museum nan Eilean in Francis Street is well worth a visit to see its displays on local archaeology

Martin Lawrence

Aerial view of Stornoway Harbour, Lews Castle in the background

and history. There are periodic exhibitions of artefacts on loan from other museums. The **Public Library** in Cromwell Street has a good collection of local books for reference.

Built in 1794, **St Columba's Parish Kirk** is one of the oldest buildings in the town. **St Peter's Episcopal Church** has an eclectic selection of artefacts including a sandstone font originally from the chapel on the Flannan Islands, a Dutch bell dating from 1631, a prayer book which belonged to the 19th century missionary David Livingstone and finally the 1608 "Breeches" bible.

The lighthouse at **Arnish Point** was first lit in 1852 and is unusual in that it was prefabricated on the Clyde rather than being built on site. The oil platform yard was built during the 1970's, but now lies idle, however if oil developments take place to the west it may see work again. There are also proposals to build aerogenerators here.

There are interesting gun emplacements from WWII on the seaward side of the Point. Two six-inch guns in a setting at Battery Point next to the power station commemorate the many volunteers who trained here over the years (NB433322).

A cairn above Arnish Point commemorates the visit by Bonnie Prince Charlie in May 1746 when he was attempting to get a ship to France. He did not succeed and in fact was not even allowed into the town.

The War Memorial on *Cnoc an Uan* (NB418343) was opened in 1924 to honour the 1,151 Lewismen killed in WWI out of a total of about 6,700 serving in the forces. It is no wonder that returning servicemen were determined to have land to themselves. This site was chosen because all four Lewis parishes are visible from it The Memorial also commemorates the 376 killed in WWII.

The return of servicemen was to

be made even more tragic by the loss of the Admiralty yacht, *Iolaire* on 1st January 1919. The vessel struck the Beasts of Holm, off Holm Point, only about 3km from Stornoway and 205 Lewismen were lost within sight of home. That 71 survived was due to a Nessman who managed to swim ashore with a line. There is a memorial to those lost at Holm Point (NB444305) which overlooks the seemingly innocuous rocks. A footpath now runs to this site.

Sir Alexander MacKenzie, who was a partner in the North West Company, was born in the town in 1764. He was the first European to travel across Canada overland, and the Mackenzie River is named after him. Another Mackenzie, born in 1752, became Surveyor General of India and was responsible for the first maps of parts of the subcontinent.

Captain Fresson first landed his Dragon Rapide on the then golf course in 1934, which was developed as an airfield in WWII for Coastal Command. Anti-submarine, anti-shipping and convoy escort patrols took place from here and many American aircraft passed through on their way to Britain. From 1986 to 1993 Stornoway was a Forward Operating base for NATO and the runway was greatly extended. Although no longer a NATO base the airfield has benefitted greatly from the military investment. A large new passenger terminal was opened here in late 2001.

The area has probably welcomed incomers since long before the first Viking entered Stornoway Harbour in the late 700's AD. Over the centuries fishermen and seamen from Holland, Scotland, Norway, the Baltic and further afield have used the port. *"High heid yins"* and ordinary folk have come and gone, and some have had streets named after them, or plaques mounted for them. Stornoway is a unique place, Gaelic yet English, Hebridean yet Scottish, laid back yet bustling.

Stornoway makes a good base from which to explore Lewis and Harris with a wide range of quality accommodation, places to eat and drink and interesting shops. Hotels include the **Royal Hotel**, centrally located on Cromwell Street (STB**HOTEL 01851 702109), the **Cabarfeidh Hotel** at Manor Park (STB***HOTEL 01851 702604) which is attractively sited on the edge of town near the Castle grounds (it also has the best restaurant in town). and the **Seaforth Hotel** (STB** 01851 702740), which is also central, near the ferry terminal.

Point Street and Francis Street

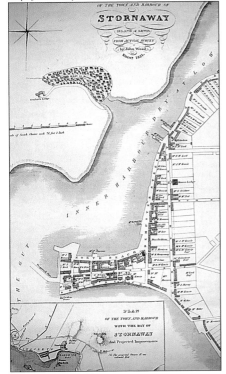

Map of Stornoway in 1821

WHAT TO SEE AND DO IN AND AROUND STORNOWAY

Lews Castle grounds - woodland walks
Chambered cairn and panoramic viewpoint at Cnac na Crioch (Gallows Hill) in Lews Castle grounds (NB417323)
Priest's Glen stone circle (off Laxdale Lane NB411352)
Memorial to Bonnie Prince Charlie, Arnish (NB425300)
An Lanntair Arts Centre
Museum nan Eilean
Stornoway Public Library
Lewis Sports Centre
Harbour area
Dun on Loch Arnish (NB189412)
Arnish Point - lighthouse and WWII gun batteries
War Memorial, and viewpoint
Mudflats and Sands of Tong for birdwatching
Lewis Loom Centre, 3 Bayhead
St Columba's Church, Aignish (NB484323)
Souterains at Gress NB491415 and NB494419
"Land Wars" cairns at Gress and Aignish

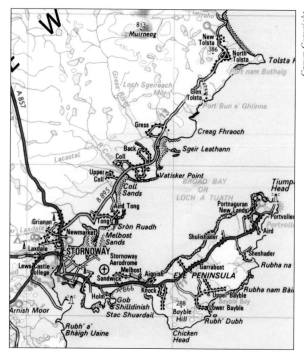

holds large numbers of seaducks and divers in winter.

Eaglais na h-Aoidhe, the roofless 14th century church at Aignish, is dedicated to St Columba, although an earlier 6th century chapel may have been founded by St Catan. There are two interesting grave slabs in the church - one to the 15th century Roderic II and the other to his daughter, Margaret, wife of the last Abbot of Iona. The nearby Crofters' Cairn commemorates the events of 1888.

The Eye Peninsula is quite densely populated with many crofts and two small harbours at Pabail and Port na Giuran. The seemingly oddly named **Chicken Head** (ON *Kirku Ness* - Church Ness) has a large Kittiwake colony.

Tiumpan Head is the most easterly point on Lewis, with expansive views across the Minch on a clear day. The lighthouse was first lit in 1900 and was made automatic in 1985. This and other vantage points along the Eye coastline are good places to watch for Risso's and other Dolphins in late summer, as well as for migrant birds in Spring and Autumn.

Prehistoric sites include Dun Bayble (NB516305) and Clach Stein (NB517318) both near Bayble and a chambered cairn (NB524331) near Garrabost. The famous Sulaisiadar axe (p19) was found in peat near the township and dates from 3150BC.

To the east of Stornoway lies the peninsula of **Aignish** or **Eye** (ON *Eggnes* - Ridge Ness) and also known as Point, which is joined to the rest of Lewis by a sandy tombolo. The north side is *Traigh Mealabost* (ON *Meal Bolstadir* - Sandy Farm) and to the south lies *Braigh na-h-Aoidhe* - both good for walks and birdwatching.

The **Tong** saltflats, which can be accessed from *Steinis* (ON *Stein Nes* - Stony Point NB448339) are good for waterfowl and waders, and there is a large Tern colony at Gob Steinis. **Loch Branahuie** at the east end of the Aignish tombolo is also very good for visiting and resident waterfowl. *The Braighe*, the bay to the south,

St Columba's Church, Aignish (Eaglais na h-Aoidhe) - soon to be renovated

Tiumpan Head Lighthouse, first lit in 1900 (Rubha an T-Tiumpan)

North-east of Stornoway are the townships of **Tong, Coll, Back, and Gress.** The fertile sand-stone soil with beaches backed by dunes and machair make this good agricultural land which was the scene of much unrest during the "Land Wars".

St Olav's Church (*Teampall Amblaigh* - NB490416) is one of the few extant chapels dedicated to a Norse saint in the Western Isles. This is not surprising considering that the Norse would have settled the best land first. The words Back, Coll and Tong are Norse (ON *Bakki* - Ridge; *Kula* - Hill; *Tunga* - Spit of land).

Further north the road rises before descending into **Tolsta** (ON *Tolis Stadir* - Tolly's Farm). There are wonderful panoramic views from here on a clear day. The beaches and low cliffs of Tolsta are among the most spectacular in the Western Isles.

Traigh Mhor is over 2km long, backed by dunes and machair, while **Traigh Gheardha** has spectacular small rock stacks or castles. The smaller **Traigh**

Loch Braigh na h-Aoidhe - south side of Aignish tombolo

Giordale makes a fine walk too. There are several natural arches and small stacks around Tolsta Head.

North of Tolsta the road peters out at the "Bridge to Nowhere". During Leverhulme's time on Lewis it was planned to build a road connecting Tolsta with Ness. However only the rather elegant concrete bridge over the River Garry was built. The coastal and moorland walk from Tolsta to Ness is however well worth the effort. Red-throated Divers, Great Skuas, Peregrines, Golden Eagles and Gannets may all be seen in this area.

Garry Beach (Traigh Gheardha) has several dramatic small rock stacks - there are remains of a defensive structure on the stack on the right

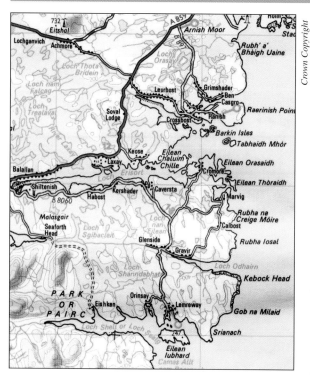

Panoramic view from Eitshall (223m) over

well worth a visit, while scattered crofting communities provide a contrast to the otherwise rather barren landscape.

Dun Cromor is a ruined Iron Age galleried dun on an islet connected to the shore of Loch Cromor by a causeway (NB402207). The gallery is clearly visible, and the north part of the islet is enclosed by a wall.

The promontory of **Pairc** is itself almost an island with only 3km of land separating Loch Erisort and Loch Seaforth. The old name for this area was **Durna** (ON *Deer Ness* - Deer Point).

The road south from Stornoway crosses the peat-covered Arnish Moor before reaching **Loch Erisort** which has a string of settlements along both shores, the biggest of which is Balallan with its attractive white-painted little post office and working crofts.

At the southern entrance to Loch Erisort is the tidal island of **Eilean Chuluim Cille**, also known as Oronsay (ON *Orfjara* - land joined to an island at low water), which has an ancient chapel dedicated to St Columba (NB385210). The dramatic and remote scenery is

One of the cairns commemorating the "Land Wars" is situated south of Balallan. In late 1887 the **"Park Deer Raid"** was organised with much publicity by crofters and cottars from Lochs. The military were called in and several of the men were tried, but acquitted. The raid was a big success in terms of publicising the situation of the people in the islands.

Loch Erisort from Balallan

from below the TV mast - one of the best easily reached viewpoints on Lewis

The hill of **Eitshall** (223m - NB305305) with its TV mast, above **Achmore** , is an excellent place from which to get a panoramic view of the well-named parish of **Lochs** and the southern part of Lewis. The water-strewn landscape is well named.

The remains of a small stone circle at Achmore (NB317292) are partly exposed by peat cuttings. This circle appears to be about 41m in diameter and may have had up to 22 monoliths in all.

On the A858 Pentland Road across the peatlands from Achmore to Stornoway there are many stumps of ancient trees which have been discovered under the peat and which would have succumbed to the advance of the peat bogs in the Bronze Age, only to be preserved under the acidic covering of vegetation, before finally being revealed again in peat cutting operations. The **refuse tip** (NB393343) at the Stornoway end of this road is a good place for birdwatchers as it attracts many gulls.

Balallan (Baile Ailean) Post Office

Dun Cromor is quite well-preserved, but its causeway is submerged

Clipping sheep in Park (Pairc)

Crown Copyright

The Standing Stones and chambered cairns of the **Callanish** area on the east side of Loch Roag form one of the most remarkable Neolithic sites in Britain. The best place to start a visit to the west of Lewis is the **Callanish Visitor Centre** which has an interpretation area, an interesting shop and a cafe.

Apart from the main stone setting (NB213330) there are several other smaller, but remarkable stone circles to visit in the area, including *Cnoc an Gharraidh* (NB223326) and *Cnoc Fillbhir Bheag* (NB226328) near the A858 just before the turn off to the Visitor Centre, *Cul a Cleit* ((NB247303) about 1km off the A858 and *Ceann Hulavig* (NB230304) off the B8011 on a small hillock overlooking Loch Roag.

An unusual feature of some of the stone circles in this area is the presence of a central cairn. Excavation of the cairn at the main site suggests that it may have been in use between 2500 and 1750BC. It is unique in resembling some cairns in Orkney. The most spectacular views of the main Callanish setting are from the sea and it has been suggested that the tallest monolith may originally have been a sea marker.

On the A858 north from Callanish, the township of Breascleit has a standing stone and a chambered cairn. The ex-shore station for the Flannan Isles lighthouse, called *"Taigh Mor"* - the Big House - is situated here too. Families of the lightkeepers stayed here before automation in 1971.

Flannans shore station - the "Taigh Mor", Breascleit

Cnoc Fillibhir Bheag, Callanish

The **Doune Braes Hotel** (STB***HOTEL Tel 01851 643252) offers fine food which is served all day as well as comfortable rooms and a warm welcome.

The broch of **Dun Carloway** (*Doune Carlabhagh* - NB190413) is the most complete and spectacular of any in the Western Isles and dates from perhaps the 1st century BC. In common with many other such brochs it is prominently situated on a small hillock overlooking the township. The walls still reach more than 9m in height.

Standing Stones of Callanish - midsummer sunrise

The double walls are over 3m thick at the base and enclose galleries which are accessed by a stairway. There is a scarcement 2.5m above the floor, which is 7.6m in diameter, and it has been suggested that this was the main habitation level. Many of the original stones are no doubt in the walls of the ruined blackhouses below the broch.

Dun Carloway and blackhouse - late 19th century

Dun Carloway - best-preserved broch in the Western Isles

The **Doune Broch Centre** helps visitors to better understand the monument and its history, as well as brochs in general. It has a small but well-stocked shop and interpretation displays.

The Lewissian gneiss makes excellent material for B&W photography

The stones were partially buried in peat which had accumulated since perhaps 1500BC, but were fully revealed when this was cleared in 1857. Unfortunately this action destroyed most of the archaeological evidence which may have been present. The surfaces have weathered into fantastic contours and the crystals within the rock give it a very beautiful texture, which varies with the light.

Obvious solar alignments are the equinoctial sunset, and local noon, but other alignments are quite possible. It has also been suggested that the eastern row is aligned with the rising of the Pleiades around May Day, or Beltane, which would have been about when crops were planted.

The 13-stone ring of the main site at **Callanish** probably dates from about 2900BC, while the chambered cairn and rows may be of later date. It seems likely that the monument may never have been completed and that avenues may have been planned for all four axes.

The 33 Lewissian gneiss monoliths which form rows which radiate from the central circle are arranged like a Celtic cross, the northern avenue being slightly east of north, while the southern arm is aligned due south. The eastern and western arms in turn face south of east and due west.

The 13 monoliths in the ring may reflect the 13 year months of the lunar year. During each month moonrise and moonset vary from north to south and back due to the relative movements of the Earth and the Moon. In addition because the plane of the Moon's orbit is slightly different from that of the Earth's around the Sun, the max-

Standing Stones of Callanish - midsummer daytime panoramic view from the south east - Loch Roag is in the background

imum northerly and southerly azimuths vary over a period of 18.6 years, as does the cycle of lunar eclipses.

During this period there are major and minor "lunar standstills" when the apparent movement of the Moon stops and reverses direction. At the latitude of Callanish (58°N) the Moon just skims the horizon at its major standstill.

This phenomenon can be observed from the avenue every 18.6 years, when the Moon appears to dance along the ridge to the south which is called *"Cailleach na mointich"* - Old Lady of the Moors. It sets behind the hill to the south west, only to momentarily reappear, or "flash" in a notch just to the west in a manner very reminiscent of the sun's behaviour at Maeshowe and the nearby Watchstone before and after the solar solstice in Orkney.

In about 325BC, Pytheas the Greek circumnavigated Britain and perhaps even visited Iceland. He is indirectly quoted by the 1st century BC historian,

Standing Stones of Callanish - midsummer early morning from north

Diodorus Siculus as having *"seen a round temple on an island no smaller than Sicily while sailing around Britain"* and that *"the path of the Moon seen from this island was very low in the sky. The god visited the island every 19 years"* - the 18.6 year cycle.

The Moon was stated *"to dance from the Spring equinox until the rising of the Pleiades"*, or Beltane (May Day). It is of course impossible to confirm that Greeks visited Lewis in the 4th century BC, but it is entirely possible. It seems that Pytheas may also have made solar observations as Hipparcus later made calculations on his data, and one of the latitudes measured was the crucial 58°N at which the Moon does its dance along the horizon at its major standstill.

Whether or not the site was actually intended to have solar, stellar or lunar alignments will never be proven, but no one can visit Callanish without being overwhelmed by the confluence of sky, water, landscape and monoliths - whatever the season, weather or time of day.

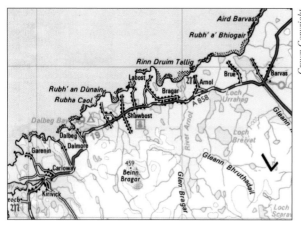

Crown Copyright

continuously settled, having ruined blackhouses intermingled with 20th century dwellings and croft buildings.

North of Carloway, the 19th century **Gearrannan** blackhouse village (NB194442) has been restored and now has a hostel, self-catering cottages, and a shop with interpretation centre and tearoom. The inhabitants were crofters and fishermen who pulled their boats up at nearby *Geodha Ruadh*.

This section of the west side of Lewis has a coastline of low rocky cliffs interspersed with beautiful sandy bays such as at **Dalmore**, **Dalbeg** and **Shawbost**. There are many small lochs, some of which are behind shingle storm beaches. Otters frequent this area, and are best seen around dawn and dusk.

The townships of **Shawbost**, **Bragar** and **Arnol** are almost

A waymarked **coastal walking route** runs from Gearrannan to Dalbeg. The trail passes two "promontory forts", which might just as easily be monastic as physically defensive, then a ruinous Norse-type mill before descending to **Dalmore** beach where a Bronze Age settlement was discovered and excavated after a big storm in 1982. Large amounts of pottery and other artefacts were recovered.

Gearrannan - restored blackhouse village near Carloway

Dalmore Beach - site of a prehistoric settlement on the machair

The walk ends at the delightful little cove at **Dalbeg** This beach is dangerous to swimmers, and surfers should take great care here. Loch Dalbeg is a good place to spot Otters and the loch has beautiful irises and water lilies in summer.

Just before **Shawbost** there is a restored Norse-type mill and barn (NB244464). This type of small mill has a vertical axis waterwheel which directly turns the millstone. Due to the noise made when in operation

Blackhouse Museum, Arnol showing byre end, barn and peatstack

Whalebone arch at Bragar

they were often referred to as "click" mills. There are many such mills in the Western Isles, but this is the only one in working order. They were in use up to the 19th century.

Shawbost also has a small but interesting **Folk Museum** in the old school, and an attractive small sandy beach. A large wool mill catering for the Harris Tweed industry is situated here.

The remains of a broch lie on a small island on *Loch an Duna* at **Bragar** which is connected to the shore by a causeway (NB286475). The broch is 16m in diameter outside and 9m inside. An internal scarcement can be made out at a

height of about 3m. Also at **Bragar** the lower jaw bones of an 85ft Blue Whale form an unusual gateway. The whale came ashore in 1920 with the harpoon which killed it still embedded in its body. The crofter who removed the explosive harpoon was lucky as it went off in his shed - luckily he was not there at the time!

The **Arnol Blackhouse Museum** (Historic Scotland - NB311493), is typical of many similar ruined buildings in the area. This development of much more ancient houses had people, animals and barn all under one roof. Smoke escaped though the thatch from the peat fire in the centre

of the living room floor. There is a small visitor centre with shop as well as a preserved early 20th century house with artefacts and decor representing an Isles dwelling of the 1940's or 1950's.

At Barvas the **Welcome Inn Filling Station** is a good place to fill up with fuel, and to buy newspapers, postcards and foodstuff. It is open long hours, but closed on Sundays. From here the A857 takes a direct route back to Stornoway across the Barvas Moor, while the same road goes north to Ness. The **Oiseval Gallery** at Brue features the photography of James Smith and is well worth a visit.

Restored Norse-type mill and barn at Shawbost (Siabost)

Loch an Duna, Bragar

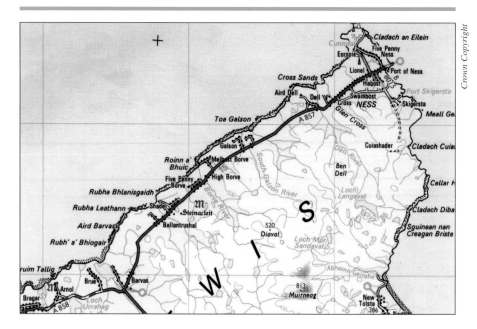

Ness (ON *Nes* - headland) is the most northerly part of Lewis. The road from Barvas to Ness runs through a series of crofting townships, making the area one of the most densely populated rural parts of Lewis. New houses, old houses, loom sheds, small shops and working crofts line much of the road, interspersed by areas of moorland.

At 5.7m high, **Clach an Truiseil** (NB376538) is the tallest monolith in the Western Isles. It may possibly be a prehistoric sea-marker. A battle between the Morrisons of Ness and the MacAuleys of Uig is said to have taken place here.

Just to the north, in Shader *(Siader)*, the enigmatic site of **Steinicleit** is probably a very ruined chambered cairn, perhaps overlain by a later domestic structure. The mound in the centre has

a kerb of stone slabs around it, while the footings of walls lead off from the site, which may have been occupied from 3000BC.

There are many old chapel sites on the west side of Lewis, most of which are close to the shore and quite ruinous. **Teampall Pheadar** (St Peter's- NB380550) is now a grassy mound above *Mol Eire* beach at *Siader*, and there is another larger *Teampall*

Pheadar at Swainbost (NB508637). **Teampall nan Cro Naomh** (Holy Cross - NB433594) at Galson was fairly complete in the 1820s, but is now collapsed.

The remains of **Teampall Ronain** (St Ronan - NB524654) lies above the cove of Stoth, a sheltered landing place east of the Butt, which is said to be the oldest chapel site in the Western

Steinicleit near Shader - probably the remains of a chambered cairn

Isles. *Port Stoth* was the main landing site for stores for the Butt of Lewis lighthouse, and for the Ness area before Port of Ness was built.

Lochruban, a rock stack off *Roinn a'Roidh* (NB507661), near the Butt, has a small bee-hive-shaped cell and legend has it that "Pigmies" lived here. It is probably a monastic cell. Ruins of similar structures exist nearby above the cliffs at *Cunndal*.

The restored **Teampall Mholuaidh** ((NB520652 - St Moluag) is said to have original-ly been built by the Vikings, and the roof timbers were driftwood from Stoth. The present church may date from the 14th century or later. There was also once a Norse castle near this church called Olvir's or Olaf's Castle. It is logical that the Vikings would settle and take control of Ness and perhaps Norse remains will be discovered in future surveys.

St Moluag's was long associated with healing of wounds and sores, however it was too holy for women to enter, particularly

Interior of Teampall Mholuaidh (St Moluag's Church), Ness

if pregnant. The people held meetings here twice a year, at Candlemas and Halloween when much eating, drinking, dancing and "dalliance" went on before the people entered the church after dark, and mass was held until morning.

It was also thought that anyone who was mentally ill could be cured by walking seven times around the church - with the sun - and then, after a drink of water from St Ronan's Well, by sleep-ing overnight in the building.

Another ancient custom in Ness

was the annual sacrifice of ale to the sea-god, *Shony*. Every house contributed *a peck of malt which was brewed into ale, and one person waded out to his waist with a cup of ale and cried out - "Shony I give you this cup of ale, hoping that you will be so kind as to send us plenty of sea-ware for enriching the ground next year".*

This was done at night and after the offering everyone went to the church which was lit by a can-dle. After the people had remained standing and quiet for a while the candle was extin-

Port Stoth - landing for the Butt of Lewis lighthouse

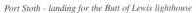

Clach an Truiseil

Isle of Lewis - *Eilean Leodhais*

Port of Ness Harbour

guished and they went outside, where the rest of the ale was consumed and the remainder of the night was spent singing and dancing.

Port of Ness has a picturesque, but silted-up little harbour from where in late summer each year a party of men depart for **Sula Sgeir**, a small rocky island 65km to the north, to harvest young Gannets or *gugas*.

The Men of Ness have always been great seamen and it used to be said that *"no Nessman of working age ever died in his bed"* -

they either lived to old age or drowned at sea. The Nessmen fished offshore using longlines and handlines from boats called *"sgoths"*, which are descendants of small boats used by the Norse, and which resemble the yoles used in Orkney and Caithness. There was a great tradition of boat building in the area, and sgoths have been renovated or even built new here recently.

Even more than in the rest of Lewis the place names are very much Norse, although the new Gaelic names tend to mask this often. There is

much attractive coastal scenery in Ness, including the lovely beach of **Buail a Muigh** at Port of Ness, the sheltered sandy cove of **Port Stoth** near the Butt, and the series of sandy beaches on the west side from **Traigh Dell** to **Eoropie**. The yellowish **Swainbost Sands** are particularly picturesque.

The sand dunes and machair are a riot of colour in summer with many wild flowers, while the cliff tops are covered in a carpet of Thrift. Although the cliffs are nowhere very high, the ancient gneiss rocks are contorted and weathered into fantastic shapes, especially at the Butt of Lewis.

The Vikings are said to have tried to tow the Western Isles back to Norway by attaching a rope to the natural arch at **Rionn a'Roidh**, however they pulled so hard that the land broke apart, leaving the trail of islands from Barra Head to the Butt of Lewis as they are now. Apparently

Houses at Lionel, Ness

Cross-slab from Rona

the rope did not break!

There is an interesting **Heritage Centre** at Ness, with a wide variety of artefacts, photographs and things to look at. Perhaps the most interesting is the small cross-slab which is pierced with three holes and which has the figure of a man inscribed on it. This grave marker came from the cemetery on Rona, and some say that it marked the resting place of St Ronan himself.

Nearby, *Taigh Dhonnchaidh* (Duncan's House), at 44 Habost, is a new arts and music centre committed to the promotion and enhancement of Gaelic language, music and the arts The house was left to the Ness Historical Society by the late

Duncan Morrison, who was a well-known music teacher.

The headland of the **Butt of Lewis,** the most northerly point in the Western Isles, is an excellent place for seawatching. Gannets may be seen fishing, and during the migration times many birds may be seen on passage. It is also a good place to see cetaceans such as Minke, Killer or Pilot Whales, as well as Dolphins. No matter what the season, time of day or weather, the Butt always has another aspect to show.

The **lighthouse** was first lit in 1862 and it became automatic in 1988. Its 37m high red brick tower is in contrast to the rather forbidding local rocks.

Sue Blair working in the pottery

Dun Eistean (NB535651) is situated on a large rock stack off Knockaird, north-west of the Port of Ness and has for long been associated with the Morrisons of Ness. There are several ruined buildings as well as a possible perimeter wall. The mound on the seaward size is a small Norse-type castle.

Port of Ness

Butt of Lewis lighthouse at sunset

Swainbost Sands, Roinn a'Roidh in background

The clan Morrison is said to be of Norse origin and descended from Olaf the Black who became King of Man and the Isles in 1226. The Morrisons held the hereditary title of *Breive* (from G *Breitheamh* - interpreter of the law) for many generations. Although Ness may seem remote today, it was readily accessible by sea. It is said that the influence of these breives may have extended as far as the Mull of Kintyre.

Harbour View Gallery at Port of Ness exhibits original watercolours, prints and cards by artist Anthony J Barber of Highland and Island scenes. The **Morven Gallery** (NB363515) displays several exhibitions every year.

Borgh Pottery is owned by Sue and Alex Blair, and their work can be seen in the delightful showroom, next to their studio, alongside an array of other interesting gifts. Their ceramics are unique and very attractive and it is extremely hard to leave without making a purchase! Visitors are also welcome to look around the unique and interesting garden which the Blairs have established here.

At **Galson Farm Guest House** (STB****GUEST HOUSE Tel 01851 850492) Dorothy and John Russell make guests very much at home, and Dorothy's home cooking is especially memorable for residents and visitors alike.

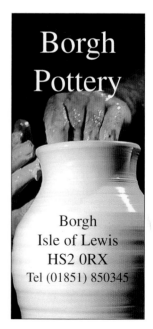

Buail a Muigh and Port of Ness from the east

Butt of Lewis lighthouse with rough sea, from the west

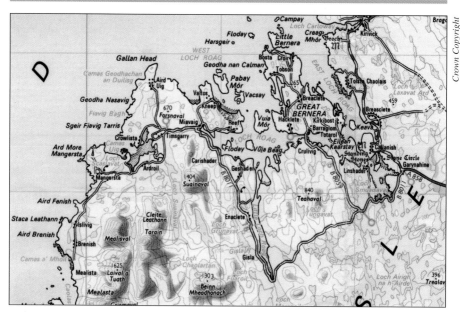

GREAT BERNERA (ON *Bjorn-oy* - Bjorn's Island) was the first of the small islands in the Western Isles to be connected to the mainland - by a pre-stressed concrete bridge, in 1953. Lobster, crayfish and crab fishing as well as fish farming are the two main economic activities. Though small, the island has much to interest the visitor.

Camas Bosta at the north end of Great Bernera

Just over the bridge and over-looking *Sruth Earshader* there are some monoliths standing sentinel over this narrow stretch of water. There are lovely views over Loch Roag from here.

Dun Baravat (NB156356) is a galleried dun dramatically situated on a small island on Loch Baravat and is signposted (about 1.5km north from the bridge.) The dun is joined to the shore by a causeway about 30m long. The northern part is over 3m high. Remains of a scarcement still exist but the interior is confused by later buildings.

At **Breaclete** the Local History Society has an exhibition and information about the island and its past in part of the Village Hall, and there is a small shop nearby.

In 1874 there was a riot on Bernera. When the sheriff-officer, Donald Munro, who was also the factor, attempted to serve writs of eviction on 56 householders, he was pelted with sods and stones. Three crofters were arrested but found not guilty when tried, but Munro was convicted of assaulting one of them whilst handcuffed and was sacked from his several public offices. A memorial cairn to these events stands north of Breaclete (NB153378).

Kirkibost Harbour

Dun Baravat on Loch Baravat - typical galleried dun

Camas Bosta, at the north end, is a beautiful sandy beach overlooking Little Bernera. Winter storms in 1992 exposed a number of structures which on excavation proved to date from the Iron Age to Norse times. Three of the houses dated from the 6th to 8th centuries AD, and have a "figure-of-eight" layout.

The houses had a large main room about 6m in diameter with a smaller room on the north side and the entrance to the south. They were built into the sand with double-skinned drystone walls. The circular shape would have resisted the pressure of the sand and also resulted in the very good structural preservation.

A replica house has been built nearby which is based on one of the excavated structures. While it is not known what the actual roof would have looked like, the reconstruction gives a vivid impression of the amount of space available in such a house.

The area around Bosta is excellent for walking, and a circular walk via *Siaram Bosta*, south along the coast and back via

Loch a'Sgail and the low hill of **Shelaval** (87m NB143391) will give lovely views on a clear day.

The ruins of a Norse-type mill lie east of Breaclete (NB168372), while slightly further on is an interesting lobster

pond on a small inlet off Loch Risay (NB173373) This was built by local people in the mid-1800's to keep their lobsters alive so that they could be sold at the best time of year for prices and survival in transit - then as now for the festive season.

Standing Stones above the bridge over Sruth Earshader

Replica Iron Age house interior at Camas Bosta

Traigh na Berie from the east with the Bhaltos peninsula on the left and Pabay Mor on the right

The B8011 to **Uig** crosses the *Abhainn Grimersta* where it enters Loch Roag. This river originates in Loch Langavat and is said to be one of the best salmon rivers in Scotland. The road passes many small lochans which are covered with Water Lilies in summer, before reaching **Gisla**, with its hydro power station and interesting Craft Shop and workshop - **Gisla Woodcraft.** The views along Little Loch Roag and Loch Roag are wild and spectacular.

Uig (ON *Vik* - Bay) is an area of great natural beauty with dramatic coastal scenery and a backdrop of mountains. The ever changing light, clean Atlantic air and proximity of the ocean all combine to impress the visitor, no matter what the season or weather.

The sandy beaches are especially varied and impressive. *Traigh na Berie* is a long sweep of sand protected by the islands of Pabay Mor and Vacsay, while the beaches at Cliff and Mangersta are much more exposed to the Atlantic swell and can be very dramatic in stormy weather.

Although Uig may seem remote today, there is plenty of evidence of past occupation. The Iron Age broch at *Loch na Berie* (NB104352) may have been of similar proportions to Dun Carloway and is preserved because it was filled by windblown sand and accumulated peat. The first floor gallery is complete and clearly shows the characteristic building techniques used.

The waterlogged nature of the site meant there was good preservation of artefacts, but also means that it is hard to view the structure. It seems that the site may have been occupied up until the 9th century AD.

Dun Bharabhat (NB099354) is on a small loch nearby and is also worth a look. It is built like a small broch, with galleried

Glen Bhaltos showing the steep, glacially scoured sides

Cnip from the south-west looking towards Pabay Mor

walls and internal stairs, but with a diameter of only 11m it was probably never very high. There are a series of "Norse type" mills on the slope leading down towards *Traigh na Berie* from here, and lovely panoramic views from the top of the hill.

A number of "wheelhouses" have been excavated in the sand dunes in the Cnip area. These were built into the sand and had radial "aisles" to support walls against the pressure of the sand. Unfortunately nothing is visible here to the visitor. The dilapidated example at Kilphedar on South Uist is similar.

Several **Viking Age burials** have been found in the sand dunes above *Traigh na Berie* which are in close proximity to earlier Bronze Age graves. One female who was in her late 30's was buried in the 10th century with a pair of distinctive oval brooches, a necklace of glass beads, a comb, and various iron tools including a small sickle. Another such burial was found in the early 20th century near *Bhaltos* school with a mixture of Celtic and Norse artefacts.

Glen Bhaltos runs from *Miavaig* to Timsgarry and was formed as a result of glacial meltwater scouring a path to the sea. The large deposits of sand and gravel at Carnish are also glacial. *Miavaig* (ON *Mjo Vik* - Narrow Bay) was once the steamer harbour and is now home to a variety of small boats as well as the shore base for fish farms.

The **Timsgarry Filling Station** is the only one for miles around, and is a good place to buy other essentials as well.

On the road towards *Ard Uig*, there is a panoramic view from *Fornaval* (205m NB061359) accessible by road. On a clear day the Flannan Islands and even St Kilda may be visible from here. Gallan Head is the site of an old military base and is now being redeveloped. The **Bonaventure Restaurant** is said to be "*a clifftop where gourmets trek to dine in splendid isolation*" by the *Glasgow Herald*. Tel 01851 672474.

On a headland called *An Bheannaich* (NB038379) about 1km west of Ard Uig village there is a small ruined chapel called *Taigh a'Bheannaich* (G the Blessing Place). A track leads most of the way to this early Christian site.

Broch at Loch na Berie

Remains of "Norse-type" mill above Traigh na Berie

Grave yard and old chapel site at Baile na Cille

The view over the wide expanse of the **Uig Sands** changes constantly as the tide ebbs and flows. Perhaps the best viewpoint is at **Crowlista** (NB040336), from where the yellowish sands combined with the mountains in the background complement each other to make a most satisfying scenic experience.

In 1831 a large collection of exquisitely carved ivory **chessmen** was discovered buried in a small stone cist in the dunes on the south side of Uig Bay. The pieces date from the mid 12th century (Late Norse Period) and are carved from Walrus ivory.

Sadly they are all in the British Museum and in the National Museum of Scotland at present.

It has been speculated that the chessmen were carved in Norway and that they may have belonged to a merchant, but as with the several silver hoards which have been found, the true story will never be known.

There is a ruined dun, **Dun Borranish**, on a small rocky knoll at the east end of the bay (NB050333) which is cut off at high tide. The sands ebb dry at low tide but are covered at high water, while the river from Loch *Suainaval* (ON *Sweyn's Hill*) winds around the east and north of the Bay.

At *Baile na Cille* there is an ancient ruined chapel in the old graveyard (NB048339) and the walls of an 18th century church make a sheltered garden for the adjacent **Baile-na-Cille Guest House** (STB**GUEST HOUSE (Tel 01851 672242), which offers a friendly welcome to visitors, and wonderful food. Although apparently remote *Baile na Cille* is a good centre from which to explore Lewis and Harris, or just the local area.

There are very fine beaches at Carnish. This area saw some of the most ruthless clearances of the 19th century when the Seaforth MacKenzies and then Matheson cleared large numbers of people from the land and shipped them to Canada to create huge sheep farms.

At **Mangersta Sands** the Atlantic never sleeps and even on a calm day there is some surf. The ancient dark rocks of the cliffs contrast with the greens and blues of the sea to create a beautiful but wild scene. A good viewpoint is ***Ard More Mangersta,*** where there is a radar station.

Further on south the townships of *Islivig* and *Brenish* are among the most remote on Lewis, but were not cleared in the 19th century. The highest hill on Lewis, *Mealsival* (574m) and the line of hills to the south dominate the scene here.

Mol Forsgeo at Mealista is exposed to the Atlantic Ocean - sometimes it is sandy and sometimes all pebbles

Traigh Mangersta from the south

Golden Eagles nest in these hills and may be seen on occasion.

At Brenish the remains of another "Norse-type mill" are in the burn on the left., while there are ruins of a fishing station at *Camas a'Mhoil*. There are also remnants from the military presence here in WWII.

Dun Borranish, Uig Sands

Taigh nan Cailleachan Dubha at *Mealista* is said to be the site of a medieval nunnery as well as another ancient chapel and graveyard (NB990243) on a small headland overlooking *Mol Forsgeo*. There are two other attractive small beaches further south, as well as a small slipway for launching boats.

Unusual croft sign

Traigh Seilebost, Harris

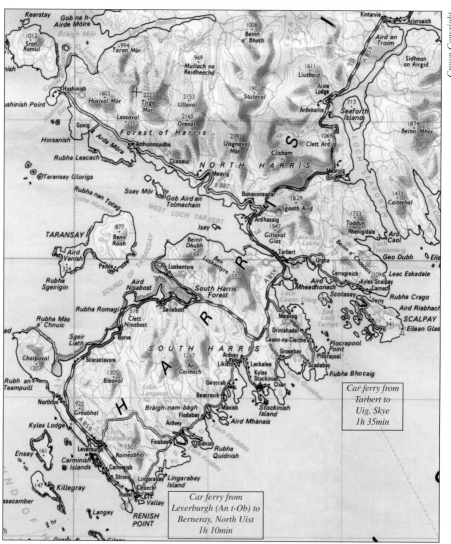

Car ferry from
Tarbert to
Uig, Skye
1h 35min

Car ferry from
Leverburgh (An t-Ob) to
Berneray, North Uist
1h 10min

Bunavoneader with Tarsaval (376m) and Sgaoth Iosal (531m) in background

HARRIS (*Na Hearadh* - possibly from ON *Herad* - Parish) is divided from Lewis by Loch Resort on the west and Loch Seaforth to the east, with Loch Langavat in the middle. The Harris Mountains complete the barrier between the two parts of the island. The split is said to date back to Norse times.

The north of Harris is mostly wild, mountainous country and ideal for hillwalkers who like exploring remote and unspoilt wilderness. Approaching from Lewis, **Loch Seaforth** divides Lewis from Harris and as the road climbs the steep hill after Ardvourlie a magnificent panoramic view unfolds along the way.

Loch Seaforth

Clisham and Allt Thomnaval

Loch Bun Abhainn-eader from Ardhasaig - Harris mountains in background

Clisham (799m) and its sisters dominate the landscape on a clear day. The remote township of **Rhenigidale** (NB229018) was only recently provided with vehicular access, and prior to that was one of the most isolated settlements in the Western Isles. An excursion into this beautiful and untamed countryside is well worthwhile, as is a brisk stroll to the top of *Toddun* (528m NB210030) for spectacular views all around.

The main road continues through the mountains before descending to West Loch Tarbert and finally reaches the village of **Tarbert** which is the main ferry port. With its range of accommodation and services this makes a convenient base to explore Harris.

Before reaching Tarbert the B887 turns off to the west, passing the abandoned whaling station at **Bunavoneader,** set up by a Norwegian company in the 1890's, to make the giant carcasses into fertiliser. After a break during WWI Leverhulme bought the facility in 1922 with the idea of making sausages for sale in Africa, however the enterprise was a failure and shut down after his death in 1925.

The road continues through wild and beautiful scenery with spectacular views over to **Taransay**, and **West Loch Tarbert**.

Sheep at Hushinish

ISLE OF HARRIS - *NA HEARADH*

Tarbert from south east with CalMac ferry, "Hebrides"

Suggested walks include taking the track north from **Meavaig** (NB101063) which leads eventually to Loch Vishimid through a remote and dramatic landscape. Further on, another track leads inland to a hydro power station and finally to the remote and deserted village of Kinlochresort. **Amhuinnsuidhe Castle** was built in 1868 by the Earl of Dunmore. Next to it is a dramatic waterfall up which Salmon leap as they return to spawn.

At the end of the road is the sandy beach of **Hushinish**. The island of **Scarp** lies just offshore to the west. A track leads north from here to **Cravadale** where there is an old fishing lodge. The golden sands of *Traigh Mheilen* (ON *Miel* - Sand) face Scarp over the shallow and often turquoise **Kyle of Scarp**.

Tarbert from the ferry

In July 1934 a German engineer, Gerhard Zucher, tried to show that rockets might be useful to deliver mail and other light supplies to isolated places. However the missile exploded on landing near Hushinish and scattered its cargo in all directions. The unique *"Western Isles Rocket Post"* covers are now much sought after by philatelists.

Nestling in its sheltered position at the head of East Loch Tarbert, **Tarbert** is the main settlement on Harris. From the ferry the bare rock which characterises so much of Harris glints in the sunshine, especially after rain. The town's steep streets and interesting shops are well worth exploring.

The **"Harris Tweed Shop"** is particularly enticing whether

one's interest is books, souvenirs, knitwear - or Harris Tweed. Several weavers premises on Harris are open to visitors, where the production process can be seen and tweed bought - ask for details at the Tourist Information Centre near the ferry terminal.

The island of **SCALPAY** has thrived in a way that few other areas in the Western Isles have. In the 1840's about 40 families who had been "cleared" from Harris and Pabbay were resettled on Scalpay.

Today most of the *Scalpachs* are either fishermen or merchant seamen, but many of the crofts are also still worked. The sheltered western bays are excellent harbours and the neat houses cluster around the shores. Catches are mostly lobsters, crabs, scallops and prawns.

At *Eilean Glas* on the east side of Scalpay is the site of the oldest lighthouse in the Western Isles, which was first lit in 1789. The present tower was built in 1824, and the light became automatic in 1978. There is a fine walk over the moor to Eilean Glas

from Kennavay (NG230950) and panoramic views from Ben Scoravick (104m - (NG237958).

Scalpay was joined to Harris in 1997 by a rather elegant steel bridge, which makes access much easier than in the past. The population of over 400 is proof that vigorous communities can survive in such apparently challenging environments.

South from Tarbert the east coast road, or **"Golden Road"** passes through **"The Bays"**. a wild and inhospitable coast where the ancient rocks are mostly bare. This area only became inhabited when the fertile machair areas on the west side of Harris were cleared for sheep farming in the 1800's. The people had to scratch a living from potatoes and oats that they grew on "lazy beds" or *feannagan* which can be seen everywhere along this coast.

Feannagan are long narrow beds of soil which have been laboriously built up using manure, domestic compost

Eilean Glas lighthouse, Scalpay

Scalpay bridge from the east

Manish on the Golden Road

Bare gneiss rocks on the east side of Harris

Traigh Iar with Taransay in the background

and seaweed as well as what turf is available. They are remarkably fertile, but very labour-intensive.

Although mostly composed of gneiss, dykes of softer volcanic rock run across Harris which date from the same time as much of Skye. Further south the landscape becomes even more bare, with exposures of red feldspar, and particularly so at **Lingerabay** where white anorthosite is exposed on the flanks of *Roinebhal*. A superquarry has been proposed to remove millions of tons of this very hard rock to make road aggregate, but the Scottish Executive have refused to let the project go ahead on environmental grounds.

Rodel with its impressive church and tidal harbour lies at the southern tip of Harris. The **Rodel Hotel** (Tel 01851 520210) has been renovated and is once again open for business. The basin next to the harbour is quite deep and visiting yachts often moor here.

In contrast to to the east coast, the west coast of Harris consists of a fringe of beautiful golden sandy beaches interspersed by headlands. The road passes though a nearly lunar landscape before the large sandy esturine beach of **Luskentyre** opens up. A series of wonderful beaches, each different from the other, and all backed by dunes and machair, follow one after the other: **Seilebost**, **Traigh Iar**, **Horgabost**, **Borve**, **Traigh Steinige** and **Scarista**. Depending on the weather, wind direction and tide they can be peaceful or violent, colourful or almost monochrome. They are always stunning.

The attractive island of **Taransay** lies off the west side of Harris. Day trips run from Horgabost beach (Tel 01859 550260). St Taran's Cross, now in the National Museum of Scotland was found at Paible. There are two ancient chapels here (NG030992), one dedicated to **St Taran** (where women were buried) and the other to **St Keith**. (where men were buried). The name *Clach na Teampall* (NG013008) suggests

Scarista Beach with Chapaval in the background

another chapel site but there are no ruins to be seen.

There are three duns, one near Paible on the coast ((NG036996), another at *Corran Raah* (NB041005) and one on *Loch an Dun* (NB022013). The south-facing sands on **Loch na-h Uidhe** is one of the finest of all the Harris beaches.

The 9-hole **Isle of Harris Golf Club** on the dunes at Scarista is in a dramatic and scenic location. Visitors are welcome, but please note that the course is closed on Sundays. Nearby **Scarista House Hotel and Restaurant** has marvellous views and serves equally fine food. Booking is essential (STB****GUEST HOUSE, Tel 01859 550238).

Bagh Steinige with rough sea

Martin Lawrence

Aerial view over Northton from the south-east - Taransay is in the background

At **Northton** *(Taobh Tuath)* there is a large area of tidal salt flats, sheltered from the west by Chapaval (339m) and Toe Head. This is one of the best places in the Western Isles to see waders, which breed on the machair, and feed on the marsh. Excavations in the machair on Toe Head have shown a sequence of occupation from Neolithic to Iron Age times. A large number of artefacts including Hebridean and Unstan Ware pottery, Beaker Ware and Iron Age burials were found. Occupation periods range from before 3000BC to after 2000BC

There is a ruined chapel at **Rubh'an Teampall** (NF970913) called *An Teampall*, which is said to have been built by the same Alasdair Crotach who built Rodel Church, in the 16th century. It is worth continuing on to the top of **Chapaval** from where on a clear day a panoramic view extends from St Kilda in the west (65km) then over the

Salt flats at Northton

Sound of Harris and on to North Uist and finally to Skye in the east (75km).

The village of **An t-Ob** (Leverburgh) was planned by Leverhulme to be a major fishing port after he abandoned the excellent harbour of Stornoway. The rock-strewn **Sound of Harris** with its fickle tides was a poor choice for such an enterprise, and on his death the project was cancelled.

There are magnificent views across the Sound of Harris from **Beinn an Toib** (103m), the hill south-east of the ferry terminal. Tidal streams in the Sound of Harris are complex, and vary between springs and neaps, day and night, and summer and winter.

The **ro-ro ferry to North Uist** runs from here. It follows a complex buoyed course between the skerries and affords one of the best birdwatching trips in the Western Isles. The **Anchorage Restaurant** near the terminal is a good place for a cup and a snack whilst awaiting the ferry.

An t-Ob (Leverburgh)

Carminish Islands and the Sound of Harris from Carminish

Breakfast, Lunch, Evening Meals	Public Telephone and Toilets
Snacks and Take-Away Meals	Facilities for the Disabled
Seating Capacity 64	and Changing Babies

The Anchorage Restaurant

Ferry Terminal	Proprietors
An t-Ob (Leverburgh)	Finlay and Mary Ann MacQueen
Isle of Harris HS5 3UB	Home Tel 01859 520291
Tel 01859 520225	

Entering the Sound of Harris from the east on a Summer's morning

St Clement's Church, Rodel from south-east

St Clement's Church at Rodel ((NG467832) is a splendid 16th century church which stands out partly as it is the only medieval building of any size to survive in the Western Isles. It was built on a rocky knoll overlooking Loch Rodel by Alasdair *Crotach* (humpback) MacLeod, of Harris and Dunvegan, who died about 1547.

The church was established in the 1520's and probably complete by the 1540's. It is about 25m long with a 30m tower at the west end and is built of local gneiss with sandstone detailing, which is said to come from Carsaig on Mull. The tower is decorated with a corbelled string course half way up with sculpted panels on each wall face.

On the north is a bull's head, on the west a figure, who may represent St Clement, with a bull's head at his feet, and on the east a woman who is exposing her genitals, and holding a child. This type of decoration is called *Shiela-na-gig* and was common on early Irish churches. It may be that the charms of the *Shiela-na-gigs* were intended to distract the the evil so that the faithful could carry on with their devotions free from Earthly temptation. The west wall panel depicts two males, one in a kilt, and the other in jerkin and hose in a suggestive pose.

Restored in 1784, and again in 1787, after being damaged by fire, the church was last renovated by the Dunmores in 1873, and is now maintained by Historic Scotland.

The building is approximately 20m by 5m inside with arched entrances to the transepts, the north being decorated with schist, the south with sandstone. On the south wall of the nave is the tomb of William MacLeod, son of Alasdair *Crotach,* who died in 1551. This tomb was badly damaged by the 1786 fire, but

Alasdair Crotach's elaborate tomb dates from the 16th century

Detail - bishops and hunting scene

the date 1539 can still be seen.

The tomb of Alasdair *Crotach* is said to be one of the best such sculptured tombs to survive in Scotland. Nine carved panels are arranged between an upper moulding and the recessed arch which encloses the tomb. The centre panel represents Christ on a cross, while the other panels represent the apostles.

The recessed interior under the arch has three rows of panels of which the top three are angels. The centre five depict the Virgin and Child in the centre with panels showing bishops on either side. To the left is a castle and to the right a galley under sail. The bottom panel is a hunting scene where Satan and Michael weigh the souls of the departed. The inscription reads *"This tomb was prepared by Lord Alexander, son of William MacLeod, Lord of Dunvegan in the year of our lord 1528"*.

The north transept has a selection of graveslabs which used to cover burials in the floor. They date from the 16th and 17th centuries.

A stairway leads from the nave into the tower, the top of which can then be reached by another stair and ladders. The window at the top looks west across the Sound of Harris.

Interior from the north showing decoration of arches

16th and 17th century graveslabs to various MacLeods

Man in kilt

Shiela-na-gig

Lochmaddy from North Lee, North Uist

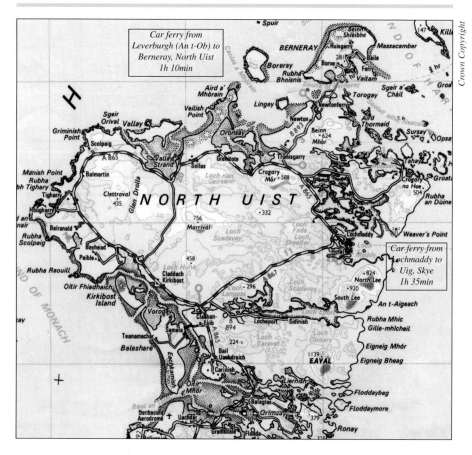

The name **UIST** may derive from the ON *vestr* - the *Vist* or *Ivist* of the Norse Sagas (West) - or it may be an older name. Originally the term applied to North Uist, Benbecula and South Uist together.

NORTH UIST is an island of contrasts. The east side is dominated by the three hills of **North Lee** (250m), **South Lee** (281m) and **Eaval** (ON Island Hill - 347m), whose distinctive conical shape features in so many views. The east side is also a maze of lochs and inlets from the sea. There are at least 120 lochs, some of which are brackish, and which cover perhaps a third of the island. Not surprisingly, trout and salmon fishing is excellent here.

The north and west coasts are fringed by magnificent sandy beaches backed by extensive machair, apart from the low cliffs at Griminish in the north west. The centre of the island is covered with peat.

The island is separated from Benbecula by *Oitir Mhor*, the **North Ford**, over which a causeway was built in 1963. The main car ferry arrives at Lochmaddy *(Loch nam Madadh)* from Uig in Skye, but there is also a small ferry from Harris which arrives at the end of the causeway to Berneray in the north of the island.

The village of **Lochmaddy** is situated in an excellent natural harbour which was used by fishermen and pirates long before the fine, but slightly incongruous, buildings of the 19th century were built. During the "Herring Boom" it was one of the main ports along with Stornoway and Castlebay for the landing and processing of catches.

The village takes its name from

MV "Hebrides" - North and South Lees in background

The Old Harbour, Lochmaddy

the two small islands at the entrance to the sea loch - *Madadh Beag* and *Madadh Mor* - the Little Dog and the Big Dog. The bay is full of small islands and skerries, and is said to have a coastline of about 70km (43miles).

The view from the top of the North Lee is magnificent and is worth the long trek across the moor. From South Lee the view encompasses Loch Eport and Eaval. Both can also be reached by small boat from Lochmaddy.

There is an interesting way-marked walk around the Lochmaddy village area which circumnavigates Loch Houram,

and also takes in several impressive 19th century buildings on the way, including the Old Court House (1827), New Court House (1875) and Bank House (1877) and other interesting sites.

The small, isolated islands, lagoons and inlets of this area make it an ideal habitat for Otters, which are often seen early and late in the day hunting for fish and eels in the ebb. The vicinity of the pier is one of the best places to start looking, for these elusive animals.

The oldest building in the village, *Taigh Chearsabhagh,* was built in 1741 as an inn and was

one of the first buildings on the island with a slated roof. It is now a very interesting local history museum and arts centre. It has a cafe and excellent shop selling local books and crafts.

The **Lochmaddy Hotel** (STB **HOTEL Tel 01876 500331) was opened in 1864 and still caters for the many anglers who come to fish the inumerable lochs each year. It is also a good base to explore North Uist from.

There is a Tourist Information Centre, Post Office and grocery shop in the village, while **"We Havitt"** and **"Island Crafts"** stock local books, artwork, crafts and knitwear.

Madadh Beag - on north side

Madadh Mor - on south side

Lochmaddy - aerial view of the Village and Old Harbour

Martin Lawrence

Loch Blashaval, west of Lochmaddy, with North and South Lees

The A865 runs north-west from Lochmaddy, passing through a strikingly beautiful landscape which is dotted with countless lochs as well as by many sites of interest. North Uist has a rich heritage of archaeological sites, ranging from the Neolithic Age to Medieval times. Most are not signposted, and many of the most interesting are not visible as they were back-filled after excavation. Luckily there are several monuments which are easily accessible and visually impressive.

Near the turn off for *Bagh a Chaise*, **Dun Torcuill** (NF888739) is perhaps the best preserved broch on the island, and is typical of the many such structures sited on small islands on lochs and accessible by man-made causeways. Although a lot of these sites date from the Iron Age and some were occupied until Medieval times, others date from the Neolithic period.

The B893 leads to the **Otternish** ferry terminal and the **Berneray causeway**. An example of a broch which was in use until Medieval times is *Dun Sticir* (NF897777), on a prominent islet on *Loch an Sticir,* near the ferry terminal. The impressive causeway is about 3m wide, and the broch about 18m in diameter. There is a later building within the structure, possibly 16th century.

Dun Torcuill showing the causeway to the shore of the loch

Dun Sticir, Port nan Long

Dun Sticir has a very substantial causeway to the shore

BERNERAY (ON *Bjornar-oy* - Bjorn's Island) lies to the north of North Uist in the Sound of Harris. Now joined by a causeway opened by the Prince of Wales in 1999, it has a rocky east side, but the west coast is one long sandy beach over 4km long, backed by a wide expanse of dunes and machair. Crofting and fishing are the main activities here, and the little harbour has a colourful array of boats.

Traigh Iar (West Beach), Berneray is nearly 5km long

There are several interesting monuments including the standing stone, *A'Clach Mhor* (NF913807), with the remains of a ruined chapel nearby. The **"Gunnery"** is a 16th century fortified building and the birthplace of Sir Norman MacLeod, a noted scholar. The roofless **Telford church** dates from 1827, and had two doors - one for the Berneray folk and the other for the Pabbay folk.

The machair is a riot of colour in Summer, with many wild flowers. It is also home to many species of waders, as well as Terns and the occasional elusive Corncrake during the breeding season. There are expansive views across the Sound of Harris from the north end. **Loch Bhrusda** is good for wildfowl

and waders. Divers and seaduck as well as Otters and Seals may be seen from the causeway or around the rocky east bays.

A'Clach Mhor

Berneray Harbour in Bays Loch is home to many small fishing craft

"The Gunnery", Baile, birthplace of Sir Norman MacLeod

Renovated blackhouse at Sollas overlooking Traigh Bhalaigh

The north coast of North Uist from *Port nan Long* to Griminish is a long series of sandy bays backed by dunes and machair. The machair and beaches at **Greinetobht** (NF825751) are especially beautiful, and it is worth the walk out to **Aird a'Mhorain** (NF832792*)* where there is an ancient cemetery. There are lovely views towards Boreray and Berneray from the long sand spit of Corran Aird a'Mhorain.

The **Udal** area has been extensively excavated - the headland was occupied from Neolithic to post-Norse times. Although there is little to see above ground, it is easy to see why the site was so favourable for settle-ment with its extensive machair, plentiful seaweed, sea for fishing and transport and the sheltered situation behind the dunes.

Sollas suffered some of the most ruthless clearances of the 19th century due to the actions of MacDonald of Sleat in Skye. Land which had been continuously inhabited for millennia was cleared of its people so that the "landowner" could make short term profits from sheep farming.

The tidal island of **Vallay** (ON *vadill* - ford) was home to the antiquarian Erskine Beveridge, who lived in Vallay House in the early part of the 20th century. He did much early archaeological work in the area..

Excavations at **Eilean Domhnuill** on Loch Olavat (NF746754) showed that the site was occupied during the Neolithic Age, and rebuilt on several occasions. The houses were rectangular with central hearths. A huge amount of pottery sherds were found, including plain bowls, Hebridean Ware and Unstan Ware. The former tend to be tall bowls or jars, while the latter are shallow, open bowls. Both have characteristic patterns of decoration.

Eilean an Tighe (G Isle of the House) on *Loch nan Geireann* is not connected by a stone causeway but excavation revealed a very similar sequence to that at Eilean Domhnuill. The site has been interpreted as a Neolithic pottery workshop due to the quantity and quality of the ceramics found there.

There is a 19th century "folly" on Loch Scolpaig (NF731750), built on top of another dun while an ancient cross from *Cille Pheadar* grave yard has been used atop a 19th century memorial. (NF726744) which overlooks *Baile Mhartainn*.

Corran Aird a'Mhorain, looking towards Boreray

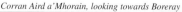

A road leads to the top of **Cleitreabhal** (133m NF749717) near the summit of which there is a chambered long cairn with an Iron Age wheelhouse built into its west end. Originally the cairn was about 30m long with an imposing facade at the east end. On a clear day there are very fine views from this hill, sometimes extending as far as St Kilda nearly 70km distant.

19th century folly, Loch Scolpaig

The **Balranald RSPB Reserve** includes beaches, dunes, machair, marsh and lochs. There is a **visitor centre** (NF718698) with good displays about the area, and where information about what currently might be seen is available. A large number of birds, especially waders and waterfowl, breed in or visit this area on migration due to varied habitat and suitable feeding grounds.

Iron Age roundhouse within chambered cairn on Cleitreabhal

Aird an Runair (NF688705) is a prime sea-watching site in Spring and Summer when the wind is onshore. The nearby Traigh Iar is very attractive to waders and is often a good place to observe migrants. In summer the machair is carpeted with an amazing mosaic of wild flowers.

Chambered cairn on Cleitreabhal

Norse era cross at Cille Pheadar

Traigh Udal, Aird a'Mhorain, looking south west

Pobull Fhinn stone circle, Langass overlooks Loch Langass and Loch Euphort, Eaval is in the background

The A867 road south from Lochmaddy to Clachan crosses an area of moorland and lochs where there is much to interest the angler, birdwatcher or archaeologist. All of the moorland bird species of the Uists may be seen here. Divers breed on the lochs, while the Langass plantation (NF845655) is good for passerines and migrants.

Raptors such as the Golden Eagle, Peregrine and Short-eared Owl quarter the moors, while Greenshank and other waders haunt the shorelines.

Bharpa Langass, the best-preserved Neolithic tomb in the Western Isles, lies on the western slope of *Beinn Langass* (NF838658) The conical exterior is 24m in diameter by 4.5m high and covers a massively constructed chamber which is intact and may be entered with care. The passage is nearly 4m long and the chamber about 3m by 2m wide and 2m high. Neolithic pottery, carved flints and some cremated bone were found here in 1911. There is a wonderful panoramic view across the moors and lochs to the hills in the west.

The nearby *Pobull Fhinn* - "Fingals People" (G *Fionn-gall* - Norseman or fair outsider) - stone circle (NF843650) is well preserved. It is oval, about 37m by 30m, and built on a levelled platform. It may originally have comprised 24 stones, the tallest being about 2.5m high. This stone setting has a dramatic outlook over Loch Langass and Loch Euphort to Eaval in the south east.

There is another stone circle to the south of the loch, *Sornach Coir'Fhinn* (NF828630) off the

Bharpa Langass chambered cairn - chamber

Bharpa Langass chambered cairn - entrance passage

B894, overlooking *Loch a Phobaill*. Several chambered cairns lie on the slopes of Cronaval and overlook the stone setting.

Nearby **Langass Lodge** (STB***SMALL HOTEL, Taste of Scotland, Tel 01851 580285) is a good place for food and drink or accommodation. A fascinating **circular walk** starts here and takes in Pobull Fhinn. The plantation and Bharpa Langass.

North of **Claddach Kirkibost**, at *Claddach a Chaolais* overlooking Kirkibost Island, the 2.6m high monolith of **Clach Mor a' Che** (G Great stone of the world) stands by the shore. Nearby there is a large but ruinous chambered cairn, **Dun Na Carnaich** (NF768663), which has several orthostats still standing.

The Claddach Kirkibost Centre in a renovated school has a cafe with lovely views to the west, a small shop and childcare facilities. It holds regular demonstrations of traditional activities as well as various cultural events (seasonal opening).

The hill of **Unival** (140m NF802673) offers wide panoramic views over the flat vista of sea, sand and shore to the west and south with lochs and hills to the east - which are always dominated by the sky. On the south-west side there is a chambered cairn, **Leacach an Tigh Chloiche** (NF800669). Several of the kerb stones remain standing, but most of the cairn has been robbed out.

Bharpa Langass chambered cairn, and view to the west

The **"Committee Road"** leads across the moors from north of Claddach Kirkibost to Malacleit.. It was built to provide work during the potato blight famine of the 1840's. There are several cairns and standing stones on the slopes above the road, while Maireabhal (NF808700 - 230m) is another excellent vantage point. There are also good views over North Uist from the road itself.

Clach Mor a'Che

Claddach a'Chaolais chambered cairn

Bharpa Carinish is one of the largest chambered cairns in the Western Isles - Eaval is in the background

Baleshare (G *Baile Sear* - East Township) is so-called because the land to the west - *Baile Iar* - was lost to the sea in a great storm in the 17th century. This area of dunes backed by machair is another good place to watch waders and waterfowl.

Just off the main road at

Thatched cottage at Cladach Chairinis

Carinish, is the ruin of *Teampall na Trionaid* (G Temple of the Trinity - NF813607) which is said to have been founded by Somerled's daughter about 1200AD, and rebuilt by Amie MacRuari, whose son Ranald was the progenitor of Clan Ranald, about 1350. It was an important seat of learning in

Teampall na Trionaid

medieval times. The 13th century scholar, **Duns Scotus,** is said to have been educated here.

In 1601 the **"Battle of Carinish"** took place here, and is still commemorated by the "Ditch of Blood - G *Feith na fala*". A group of about 40 MacLeods from Skye had come over to lay waste to North Uist and steal cattle, some of which were in the precincts of the *Teampall* for sanctuary.

A much smaller group of MacDonalds attacked with swords, bows and arrows and after a fierce fight, the MacLeods were subdued, only two escaped to their boats which had been left at Loch Euphort.

In an example of 20th century "progress", road-widening has virtually destroyed the once-fine stone circle south-east of Carinish (NF833603), which had 15 uprights in 1915. However the nearby and spectacular Neolithic chambered cairn of **Bharpa Carinish** (NF837603) to some extent compensates for this official vandalism. At 50m long, 21m wide and 2m high and enclosing a chamber at least 6m long the cairn must have been very imposing when built.

There is a fine walk over the moors from the end of the **Cladach Chairinis** road to the summit of **Eaval** (ON *Ey fjall* - Island Hill). The route leads over the moors, passing shielings and the small **Dun an t'Siamain** (NF886595) before ascending to the summit cairn (347m) with its very impressive views.

GRIMSAY (ON *Grims-oy* - Grim's Isle) is joined to North Uist and Benbecula by the North Ford causeway which was opened in 1960 by the Queen Mother. Before this time the crossing could be hazardous due to quicksands, or getting caught out by a rapidly rising tide. This attractive small island has a circular road with many nice vistas across the fords.

Bagh Mor is particularly attractive, with views to Eaval and Ronay. The utilitarian modern fishing harbour at Kallin is base for the many small fishing boats which operate in the area.

At the eastern end of Grimsay lies the ruined Teampall Naomh Mhichel (St Michael's Chapel - NF882548) where the bodies of seamen carried ashore by the tide were traditionally buried.

Margaret MacDonald's **"Island Crafts"** is signposted at *"Cnoc Aird"*. Nearby is an excavated roundhouse.

Kallin Harbour on the east side shelters many small fishing boats

Fishermen cleaning the bottom of their lobster boat, Grimsay

Oitir Mhor and Benbecula from Grimsay

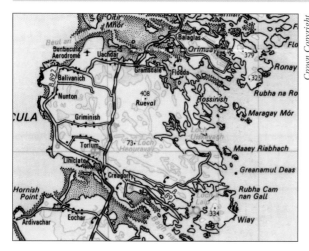

The much ruined remains of two chambered cairns lie north of *Loch nan Clachan* (NF813527).

Of several duns, **Dun Buidhe** (NF793547) near Balivanich is the most impressive. Its islet is joined via *Eilean Dubh* to the loch shore by substantial causeways. The site was reoccupied in late medieval times.

A Pictish symbol stone, now in the National Museum, was found near **Strome Shunnamual.** This granite slab is incised with two enigmatic motifs. The only other such stone so far found in the Western Isles was on Pabbay, south of Barra (p126).

The only wheelhouse so far known on Benbecula is now under one of the runways of the airport, and to date no Pictish or Norse domestic site has come to light, making the carved stone even more enigmatic.

BENBECULA (G *Beinn na Faoghla* - the Hill of the Fords) lies between the two Uists and is largely flat but dominated by the low hill of **Rueval** (124m) from which there is an excellent view of the island and the Fords.

The island is studded with many lochs. The west side has extensive sandy beaches with a wide machair plain, while the east coast is mostly rugged and backed by moorland. In WWII an airfield was established at **Balivanich** (G *Baile a Mhanaich* - "Monkstown") which continues to be used by the military as part of their Hebrides Rocket Range, as well as by civilian traffic. The connection to South Uist was completed, as a concrete bridge, to facilitate the import of supplies during WWII and upgraded to the present causeway in 1983.

There is much of archaeological interest on the island. At **Gramsdale**, near the North Ford, there are several standing stones (NF825562 and 825553). The northern site has one upright and nine fallen monoliths, while there is one upright and two fallen stones at the southern one.

Although nothing remains of the monastery at Balivanich, the remains of an ancient chapel, **Teampall Chaluim Cille,** dedicated to St Columba (NF783549), and its associated well, *Tobar Chaluim Cille*, remain on the south east side of the village. Another old chapel at **Nunton** (Nun's Town) (NF768538) may date from the 14th century. There was a nunnery in this area, but this declined after the Reformation. It is said that its stones were used to build Clanranald's new house and steading in the 18th century. **Nunton Steadings** have now been renovated

Nunton chapel

Beach below Balivanich Airport

Gramsdale standing stones, Eaval in the background

Pictish symbol stone

Borve Castle (NF773506) is said to have been built by Amie MacRuari in the 14th century and it was the Clanranald base for many years until Ormiclate Castle was built on South Uist. Little now remains of this once

imposing building or of the nearby **Teampall Bhuirgh.** The name *Borve* suggests that there may have been a ruined broch here in Norse times.

For birdwatchers the west coast

beaches, machair and lochs are good places to view waders, wildfowl, and gulls. **Culla Bay** and **Poll na Crann** or "Stinky Bay" - so called because of the smell of rotting seaweed which often pervades the beach - are

Cattle grazing on machair fields near Borve

Wild flowers on the machair near Nunton

The west coast of Benbecula at low tide with South Uist in the background

Borve Castle was the base of the Clanranalds for centuries

especially attractive to waders in migration times. The drain from *Oban Liniclate* (NF785498) and the lochs nearby are particularly good for migrants.

The rugged east side of the island can be very rewarding to the energetic. The track which leads to Rueval from the **Market Stance** (NF806537) also leads to the remote but beautiful **Rossinish** peninsula, Scaralode and *Loch Uisgebhagh*. It was in this area

that **Bonnie Prince Charlie** was hidden for much of his time while on the run in 1746.

The sandy beaches backed by machair and dunes on the north side of Rossinish (NF873538) as well as several other locations around *Loch Uisgebhagh* are unusual for their east coast situation. All are beautiful and unspoilt. Otters frequent these shorelines, which, although only a few miles from "civilisation", give the feeling of being far from

anywhere.

The lack of a deep water harbour on Benbecula meant that goods were landed at Loch Skipport in South Uist and then trans-shipped by small boat, but in the 1890's the Congested District Board built **Peter's Port** on the south-east extremity of the island. This typical example of official folly initially had no road to it and the approach is hazardous for vessels of any size and thus was little used.

In the 20th century the presence of the military has done much to boost the economy of the island. Today Benbecula is the centre of administration for the Uists and Barra, while there is a fine new Community School and Museum at **Liniclate.** Balivanich has several interesting shops to visit.

Benbecula Golf Course has 9 holes, and is on the machair to the north east of the airport, and though flat has plenty of man-made and natural hazards.

Creagorry Hotel (STB*HOTEL Tel 01870 602024) and the **Dark Island Hotel** (STB**HOTEL Tel 01870 603030), are in the south of the island. The excellent **Stepping Stones Restaurant** in Balivanich is also well worth a visit (Tel 01870 603377).

MacGillivrays, is particularly to be noted for its superlative selection of books on Hebridean and Scottish subjects, which was described as "wonderful" by Norris MacWhirter of the *"Guinness Book of Records"*.

The North Ford in the mist

BONNIE PRINCE CHARLIE

After the "Glorious Revolution" of 1688 when William of Orange became King of Scotland and England, James VII and II fled to France. There were abortive rebellions in 1679 and 1715 in favour of James, the "Old Pretender" and in 1745, of "Bonnie Prince Charlie", or the "Young Pretender - all of which were unsuccessful.

Prince Charles Edward Stuart landed at the Princes Strand on Eriskay on 23rd July 1745 before raising his standard at Glenfinnan on 19th August and marching south via Edinburgh to Derby before retreating north again. After a lucky victory at Falkirk the Jacobites then occupied Inverness, but were utterly routed by the Duke of Cumberland's much superior Government forces at Culloden on 16th April 1746.

With a reward of £30,000 for his capture, Bonnie Prince Charlie went on the run and ended up in Benbecula on 27th April 1746 after a wild crossing of the Minch. He and his companions were to spend the next few months as fugitives on South Uist, Lewis and Benbecula.

Despite the price on his head and local knowledge of his hiding places, he was not given up to the authorities, and finally escaped to Skye from Rossinish in Benbecula, with the help of Flora MacDonald, who was born at Milton in South Uist.. Lady Clanranald of Nunton House was a key player in organising this.

Whether the Government actually really wanted to catch him, or merely ensure his departure from Britain is not clear, but there are many stories about his short time in the Western Isles as a fugitive. He eventually left for France on 20th September 1746.

Flora MacDonald was briefly held in the Tower of London, where Samuel Johnston, and others, visited her, before she married and emigrated to Carolina. Her husband fought on the British side in the American War of Independence, and she died in Skye in 1790, where she is buried.

The main effects of the rebellion were the hastened decline of the traditional clan system and the rapid development of commercial "landlordism" which together were to lead to the clearances, emigration and the establishment of the crofting system.

One of the Prince's companions was Neil MacEachan who had fled to France with him. The son, James, was to rise to fame under Napoleon. He became a Marshall

Flora MacDonald's birthplace

in the French army and he visited his father's birthplace at Howmore in 1826.

Surprisingly, the Prince's less than illustrious life in exile, mostly chasing ladies it seems, appears to have done nothing to reduce the myth and romance of the '45, which in reality was brutal and ill-planned. It certainly had very little to do with the welfare of the people of the Highlands and Islands

Boeing B-17 Flying Fortress off South Uist

After all the social changes and upheavals of the previous 200 years, the mid 20th century saw much further development, this time due to wartime necessity. During the 1930's Balivanich was one the grass strips used by the De Havilland Rapides of Scottish Airways to provide the first regular air services to the Western Isles. With war looming it was clear that air bases would be needed as far west as possible for anti-submarine and convoy protection work.

The Benbecula runways were built by laying bitumen directly over sand which had been compacted. The resulting slightly flexible surface was not ideal, but was usable by the aircraft of the era due to their relatively low ground pressure.

Work on the South Ford road link actually began in 1938, while construction of the airfield started in 1940, and it became operational in August 1941. Although there was some local concern about the possible loss of traditional Gaelic culture due to the influx, the RAF personnel were made very welcome.

In late June 1942, 206 Squadron became operational on anti-submarine duties, with Hudsons which were soon replaced with B17 Flying Fortresses. These heavily armed long range aircraft achieved considerable success, sinking at least 12 U-boats, but perhaps more importantly forcing the submarines to remain submerged in the area to avoid detection, thus denying

them some freedom of action. 220 Squadron, also with B17's arrived in March 1943, but both were redeployed to the Azores that October. Swordfish of 838 and 842 Fleet Air Arm Squadron were deployed under RAF Coastal Command on short range patrols in August 1944. In September 1944 Wellingtons of 179 and 304 (Polish) Squadrons arrived but despite intensive patrols they failed to find a single submarine. Finally, 36 Squadron, also of Wellingtons, was based here until June 1945.

Today Balivanich airfield is shared by civilian airlines which provide daily flights to Glasgow, Inverness, Stornoway and Barra and the military needs of the Missile Testing Range on South Uist. The continued presence of associated personnel and their

Boeing B-17 over Benbecula

WWII German U-boat on the surface - the reason for RAF Benbecula

The North Ford from Benbecula looking towards North Uist and Eaval

dependents provides work and is a boost to the local economy.

Until the building of the causeways, Benbecula was isolated at high tide and during storm surges. The crossings could be dangerous on a rising tide, in the fog, or in the dark, and were never suitable for road vehicles. In fact the first outside direct links were by air, due to the lack of a suitable harbour.

The Fords are excellent places to see waterfowl and waders. In particular the south side of the South Ford is a favourite roost for waders at high tide. The small road along the north west shore of South Uist and the eastern shore of Gualan tend to be particularly good. Care should be taken not to obstruct traffic on the causeways themselves.

There are spectacular views over the Fords from many locations, but perhaps the best are from the north end of Benbecula (NF825565) and from the layby south of Creagorry towards South Uist (NF803479). Depending on the location, season, weather and time of day there are almost limitless combinations of land, water, sand and sky for the artist or photographer to interpret. The fords can be dangerous on foot - take care!

Car ferry from
Lochboisdale to
Castlebay 1h 20min
Oban 4h 50min (direct),
via Castlebay 6h 40min

Car ferry from
Eriskay to
Barra
50min

SOUTH UIST *(Uihbist a Deas)*, the largest of the Uists, is another island of contrasts, with a mountainous east side and rocky east coast indented by several large sea lochs and facing the deep waters of the Minch. The west side has an almost continuous sandy beach faced with dunes and machair land behind, giving way in turn to peaty moorland. The whole west side of the island is dotted with innumerable lochs and lochans.

There are many sites of archaeological and historical interest on South Uist, ranging from Neolithic tombs and settlement sites to Iron Age duns and wheelhouses to medieval chapels. While some are signposted, most are not and many are in a state of disrepair or neglect.

In Spring and Summer the extensive machair is covered with a carpet of wild flowers and grasses and is home to many breeding birds, especially waders. The elusive Corncrake also still holds on in this area. The moorland is home to breeding Hen Harriers and Short-eared Owls, with Divers on the remoter lochans, while Golden Eagles and Peregrine Falcons breed in the craggy mountainous areas

The north end is dominated by **Loch Bee**, a large, shallow loch which is open to the sea at high tide, and thus slightly brackish. There is a large resident population of Mute

Loch Bee looking south-east to the hills

Croic a Deas, Ardvule, west coast looking towards Kildonan

East coast from seaward - Ushenish with Hecla and Beinn Mhor

Drimore from Rueval - coastal machair plain, lochs and west coast

Swans on the loch, many of which are non-breeding. The outlet to the sea at **Clachan** (NF770465) is a particularly good place for waders and wildfowl.

North Bay (NF748459), **Ardivachar Point** and nearby *Loch an t-Saile* are all good places to look for migrants. Greenland White-fronted Geese also sometimes winter here. The nearby shop and workshop of **Hebridean Jewellery** at Iochar is well worth a visit.

Along the Iochar road a number of traditional thatched houses lie in various stages of decay. Some are now being renovated, but most are steadily reverting to nature.

Loch Carnan is the first of several long indentations in the east coast of South Uist. **Orasay Inn** (STB**INN, Tel 01870 610298) offers comfortable accommodation, and fine *"Scottish Natural Cooking"*, prepared by chef Isobel Graham.

Salar Salmon, at Lochcarnan, makes the unique and award winning *"Flaky Smoked Salmon"*. and other delicious

fish products. These are available in many shops in the islands.

South of Loch Bee **"Our Lady of the Isles"**, by Huw Lorimer, (NF777408) was erected in 1957 to guard the island against any ill effects from the nearby Royal Artillery establishment. There is a marvellous view from here across the machair plain to the west coast and to the Atlantic Ocean beyond.

Loch Druidibeg National Nature Reserve encompasses most of the habitats of South Uist, stretching from the Atlantic coast almost to Loch Skipport in the east. Apart from during the breeding season, when part of the reserve is closed, visitors have free access. There is a self-guided walk through part of the area. The Reserve is an important breeding site for Greylag Geese which, unusually for UK, are resident here. There is a good example of a dun on the south side of the loch (NF778371).

Our Lady of the Isles

Derelict thatched "white house" (Taigh Ban)

Loch Skipport has a dilapidated pier from the Herring boom times, and is a good point from which to start a walk to **Hecla** (606m) or the remote headland of **Ushenish**, with its lighthouse, which was first lit in 1857, and has been automatic since 1970.

The beautiful glacial valleys of Glen Ushenish, Glen Corrodale and Glen Hellisdale are well worth the effort of the long walk. In particular the 260m high sheer craigs of **Coire Hellisdale** (ON *Hellis Dale* - Cave Valley) on the north-east face of ***Beinn Mhor*** (620m) are spectacular, especially early on a summer's morning.

Bonnie Prince Charlie spent several weeks in 1746 hidden in the Glen Corrodale area to evade the authorities. **Prince's Cave** (NF835313) is reputed to be one of his hiding places. Although they did not overtly support him during his campaign, the local clan chiefs, Lochboisdale and Clanranald, assisted his evasion of and subsequent escape from the authorities.

Remote Ushenish lighthouse on the east coast has no access by road

Loch Druidibeg (National Nature Reserve)

Dun Altabrug - on an islet in a loch and joined to the shore by a causeway

There is a tall **standing stone** (NF770321) nearly 3m high above Stoneybridge, which can be reached by road leading to a water pumping station, from where there is a panoramic view of the west side of the island. This is a good point to start a climb to the tops of Beinn Mhor, Beinn Corradail and Hecla.

Nearby, **Dun Altabrug** (NF769344) is quite well pre-

served and may be reached by its causeway from the loch shore. Other dun sites include **Dun Uiselan** (NF777454), at the north end, and *Dun Mor* (NF776415), north of Rueval. *Caisteal Bheagram* (NF761371) on Loch an Eilean, near Howmore is a small ruined tower with several small windows which may be 14th century. There are ruined longhouses around the tower and the site

may have been in use by Clanranald until the 17th century.

At **Howmore**, there are ruins of two chapels and two churches, the oldest of which may be 13th century, although there are suggestions that this was a much earlier Christian settlement site. *Teampall Mor* (St Mary's) is quite large, 20m by 8m, and the east gable with two windows survives, while the other church is smaller and dedicated to St Columba.

The chapels are much smaller, and have inwardly-inclined door jambs and steep gables reminiscent of early Irish practice. A third chapel was destroyed about 1866. An armorial stone of Clanranald from this site is now in the nearby **Kildonan Museum**. This stone disappeared from Howmore in 1990, but was "rediscovered" in London in 1995.

Ormiclate Castle (NF740318) was built for Ailean, chief of Clanranald in 1701, and burnt down in 1715, due to a kitchen fire, the day after its owner was killed at the abortive battle of Sherriffmuir. The gaunt ruin was never rebuilt, but its still-

Chapel at Howmore

Teampall Mor, Howmore

Clanranald stone, Howmore

standing gables attest to the quality of its construction, if not the success of its occupant.

Loch Einort almost splits South Uist in two, and indeed many of the machair lochs drain eastwards into it. At *Airidh nam Ban* (G Shieling of Women), there was once a nunnery. Later there was an inn here. This is a good departure point for exploring the surrounding hills.

Allt Bhogalair (NF800290) is a small river running off Beinn Mhor, in whose lower valley a small but very impressive native woodland persists. The steep-sided ravine protects the rich flora from grazing. Although mostly composed of Birch and Hazel, there is an amazing diversity of flora here. The best times to visit are from May to August.

Caisteal Bheagram, Loch an Eilean, Drimsdale

Stoneybridge standing stone

Rubha Ardvule - headland on west side - excellent sea watching site and westernmost point of the Western Isles

Rubha Ardvule is the most westerly point in the Western Isles, and is an excellent place from which to watch birds on passage during migration times. **Dun Vulan** (NF714297) is on the south side of the peninsula leading to Rubha Ardvule and was partially excavated during the 1990's as it was being steadily eroded by the sea. The original broch was built directly on sand and thus seems to have partially collapsed soon after construction. The bottom 4m of the tower has been preserved under the shingle of a storm beach, and excavation revealed the first floor, the lintelled entry passage, collapsed stairs and internal wall galleries.

Detailed studies of the extensive midden have produced much interesting information about the life style of the people who lived here in the first centuries AD. The main floor of the original broch remains unexcavated. The site was occupied for several hundred years, perhaps from 200BC until 400AD.

There is much evidence of ancient habitations on the machair in this area, which seems to have been the main centre of population until about late Norse times, when this moved inland to the "black-lands", the area between the machair and the peat bogs.

An Iron Age wheelhouse was excavated in the area in 1952, and another more recently found example has been reconstructed at the Kildonan Museum, which is situated in the old Kildonan School, now renovated. Apart from its informative displays, there is a cafe and craft shop.

Dun Vulan

On the west side of **Upper Loch Kildonan** (NF732283) there is a series of interesting ruins which comprise a large and impressive 12th century Norse church with a semi-circular apse at its east end and associated domestic buildings. There are also remains of several rectangular buildings on the nearby Eilean Mor, which is connected to the shore by a now-submerged causeway.

Kildonan 12th century Norse church

There are strong similarities between this site and Finlaggan on Islay, the base of the Lord of the Isles in the 12th century, and Kildonan may have been an important Viking settlement. Eilean Mor could be be the *"Tingwall"* or Norse parliament of the Uists.

Although a Viking Age settlement was found at Udal on North Uist, and a single house at Drimore on South Uist, typical Norse-style rectangular houses have until recently been notably absent from Western Isles discoveries. However, nine Viking houses have now been excavated near *Trollaskeir* (ON *Trollr sker* - Troll's Skerry - NF724275)) which date from the 11th century or earlier.

Flora MacDonald, who helped with the escape of Bonnie Prince Charlie from the Western Isles, was born at Milton in 1722, the daughter of the local tacksman. There is a commemorative cairn on the site of the house which is said to be her birthplace (NF742269).

Near **Kilphedar** (NF733203) another **aisled wheelhouse** was excavated in the 1950's on the machair. Built into the sand, its circular stone wall is nearly 9m in diameter, with 11 drystone radial piers each with a space or "aisle" separating it from the outer wall. The central hearth can still be made out, while the entrance passage runs in from the east. This is the only such excavated wheelhouse in the Western Isles which has not been back-filled, but it is in a sad state of neglect.

Reineval chambered cairn showing surviving kerb stones

Of the several Neolithic chambered cairns on South Uist, the most spectacular is on the north side of **Reineval** (NF755259). This well-preserved tomb overlooks the fertile coastal plain and lochs of Milton and Frobost. It is about 21m in diameter and 4m high with large kerbstones still in place while some of the orthostats of the entrance remain on the south-east side and the chamber may still be intact.

stones are still in place, and the corbelled roof of the chamber is undamaged.

In *Cladh Hallan*, the cemetery near Loch Hallan (NF734219), there is a 16th century carved grave slab, perhaps originally from Howmore, or more likely associated with the ruined church on this site, which is typical of many in the Western Isles with its coastal location.

Aisled wheelhouse at Kilphedar

The cairn at *Loch a Bharp* (NF777215), off the road to Lochboisdale is even better preserved, no doubt because of its remoteness. Situated at the north-west end of the loch, this site is well worth a visit, but beware the many burns and lochs on the way. It is about 26m in diameter and 6m high. Most of the kerb

16th century grave slab, Hallan

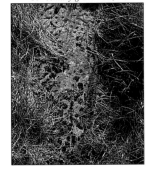

Lochboisdale aerial from the south

Martin Lawrence

Lochboisdale (*Loch Baghasdail* - originally from ON *Kastel vagr* - Bay of the Castle) - There is a ruined castle on Calvay, the small island which guards the entrance to Lochboisdale, which may date from late Norse times. Its substantial walls are nearly 2m thick and the ruins include a small tower, and foundations, all of which are reminiscent of similar structures in Caithness and Orkney.

The road to Lochboisdale was only built in the 1840's during the potato famine, just in time to assist in the forced emigration of over 1,000 people to Canada. During the Herring Boom of the late 1800's and early 1900's the port's convenient location and sheltered harbour ensured that it

was important for the landing and processing of the "Silver Darlings". Several small fishing boats still work from here today. The Calmac ferry runs from here to Castlebay on Barra and to Oban.

If time permits the walk to the top of *Triuirebheinn* (357m), is well worthwhile for the panoramic view, while the shorter route to **Beinn Ruigh Choinnich** (280m), the hill which dominates the village, affords wonderful views over Lochboisdale. The 9-hole **golf course** on the machair at **Askernish** was first opened in 1891, and although on flat machair, it has been described as *"second to none in the various elements which go to make up a really good course".*

Another good viewpoint is from the top of **Aisgerbheinn** (NF755237), which is easily reached by a track opposite the road to the golf course. There is a dramatic view over the loch-strewn area of Daliburgh and the machair plain from here.

The **Lochboisdale Hotel** (STB***HOTEL Tel 01878700332) is a traditional sporting hotel much used by the many anglers who find South Uist so attractive. Non-fishermen are equally welcome. Most of the shops are at Daliburgh, as well as the comfortable **Borrodale Hotel** (STB**HOTEL Tel 01878 700444), which is also a good place to stay, or to stop for a meal.

Two chapel names, *Cille Pheadar* (St Peter), which is said to be between the shore and *Loch Liana Moire*, and *Cille Bhrighde* (Kilbride) in the old burial ground at the south end, recall early Christian activity.

At **Pollochar**, overlooking the Sound of Barra, an isolated monolith (which may have been moved) stands sentinel on the shore (NF745144). This ancient stone might have been a sea-mark for the western approaches

Fishing boats at Lochboisdale

Daliburgh from Aisgerbheinn

to the Sound, which needs careful navigation to avoid its many skerries and sandbanks. The **Pollochar Inn** (STB***INN Tel 01878 700215) is nearby.

The picturesque southern shore road leads to **Ludag**, and then *Bagh Mor* with its expansive sandy beach and dunes. The road ends at South Glendale, but a track leads across the moor to North Glendale and the south side of Lochboisdale.

The unpolluted and extensive lochs, streams and sea inlets, and lack of fish farming and other development ensure that angling for Salmon, Brown and Sea Trout remains excellent in South Uist. The same conditions are of course also beneficial to wildlife in general.

Lochboisdale from the south - Beinn Ruigh Choinnich on right

Dramatic evening light over Lochboisdale from the ferry

Lochboisdale from North Glendale

Standing stone at Pollochar

The causeway from Eriskay to Ludag was opened in 2001

ERISKAY (ON *Eriks-oy* - Eric's Island) is a delightful small island on the north side of the Sound of Barra, and now joined to South Uist, near Ludag, by a causeway. Fishing is the main occupation here and boats are moored at **Haun** (ON *Havn* - Haven) and **Acairseid Mhor** (G Big Harbour).

Bonnie Prince Charlie made his landfall here in summer 1745 from the French ship *Le Dutillet*, on the beach on the west side which is still called **Coilleag a'Prionnsa.** He then proceeded to Arisaig on the Mainland after evading an HM frigate.

The island is colourful with wild flowers in summer, especially where the sheep cannot reach. Eriskay ponies also graze some of the land and this helps enrich the flora. These ponies are said to descend from the native Scottish ponies and may be similar to those used by the Picts and Scots in battles.

The large church at Haun was built by Father Allan MacDonald, at the end of the 19th century. He was also a noted Gaelic poet and scholar. The altar base is formed from part of a lifeboat lost off *HMS Hermes* in WWII and washed ashore, while the church bell is from the WWI German battlecruiser, *SMS Derrffliger*, scuttled in Scapa Flow in 1919.

There are pleasing views over the Sound of Eriskay and South Uist from **Beinn Scrien** (185m) and over the Sound of Barra from **Beinn Stac** (122m). Most of the houses are near the harbour at Haun, as is the pub **"Am Politician"**, which is easily recognised by its "Harrison Line" flag outside.

The famous **Eriskay Love Lilt** and many other traditional songs and folklore were recorded in the early 20th century by Marjory Kennedy-Fraser and others, which made the island's name well known and helped preserve in print much that was hitherto passed on orally.

There is a new **ro-ro ferry terminal** at the south end of *Coilleag a' Prionnsa* which provides a car ferry connection with the north end of Barra.

Altar in St Michael's of the Sea

Coilleag a'Prionnsa where Bonnie Prince Charlie landed in 1745

Memorial to Bonnie Prince Charlie

WHISKY GALORE

On 5th February 1941 the 8,000 ton Harrison Lines ship *SS Politician* accidentally hit a submerged rock off the east side of Eriskay. She was carrying general cargo to the United States which included about 21,000 cases of whisky, which, given wartime shortages and the slow response of the authorities, was like manna from Heaven to the islanders.

The "SS Politician" which went ashore off Eriskay in 1941

UNSPOKEN THOUGHTS OF A GREAT POLITICIAN

"NEVER IN THE HISTORY OF HUMAN DRINKING WAS SO MUCH DRUNK SO FREELY, BY SO FEW"

WITH APOLOGIES TO THE LATE SIR WINSTON CHURCHILL TO WHOM THIS THOUGHT MUST HAVE OCCURED AT A MOMENT WHEN BRAIN AND POWER OF SPEECH WERE NOT SOBERLY CONNECTED

With apologies to Winston Churchill

Although the ship was finally beached in shallow water and much of the cargo salvaged, the islanders succeeded in "saving" a large proportion, which was hidden in all manner of places on Barra, Eriskay and South Uist. Fishing boats from as far away as the east coast were also rumoured "to have replenished their stores".

The Customs did finally arrive and several men were arrested and convicted, though without the cooperation of the local police. The film ***Whisky Galore***, based on the book by author Compton MacKenzie, then living on Barra, was released by Ealing Studios in 1948. It used Castlebay and Barra for much of the location work, and remains a favourite comedy over 50 years later.

The remains of the wreck can still be made out at low tide on a sandbank near Calvay Island, and several bottles were recovered during the laying of the electric cable from South Uist by divers. Samples of **Polly bottles** as they are referred to can be seen at the pub - genuine articles have *No Resale Without Federal Approval* on the bottle. It is rumoured that bottles still come to light today during house renovations and the like.

"Whisky Galore" movie poster

A "Whisky Galore Polly bottle"

Acairseid Mhor

Sunset over South Uist and Eriskay from the ferry

Sunset over Barra from the ferry

Crown Copyright

Panoramic v

18th century, and burnt in 1795. It is now in the charge of Historic Scotland, and can be visited daily by a small ferry.

Castlebay was a very busy port during the **Herring Boom** of the late 19th and early 20th centuries. In 1869 James Methuen, a leading fish merchant from the east coast, started using the harbour to land and process Herring. Up to 400 boats fished out of Castlebay during the short season, and over 2,000 people arrived to cope with the gutting, salting and packing into barrels. Fishing is still a major part of the Barra economy, and several boats work out of Castlebay. The larger vessels are based at Northbay, where the Barratlantic fish processing factory is situated. Most landings are exported

BARRA (G *Barraigh*, ON *Barr-oy* - Broch Island - but it is also said to be named after the 6th century Irish follower of Columba, Finbar - St Barr). This beautiful little island encompasses the best of the Outer Hebrides - climate, clean, unspoilt environment, beaches, machair, peaty moorland, heathery hills, a wealth of archaeology, history and wildlife, as well as a thriving Gaelic culture.

The harbour at **Castlebay**, the main settlement, is one of the best in the Outer Hebrides, and is unique in retaining its castle (much renovated in the 20th century). **Kisimul Castle** (ON *Kastali Holmr* - Castle Holm) probably dates back to Norse times, but the existing structure is no earlier than 15th century. The first mention of Barra in the sagas is when Onund Wooden-Leg is said to have arrived with

five ships in 871AD and driven away the local chief, Kiarval. He then used Barra, no doubt Castlebay, as his winter base. Recent work suggests that settlement here goes back to prehistoric times.

Based on a small island, but with a very convenient fresh water spring, the site is ideal for defence, and was probably fortified long before the Vikings arrived. It was the stronghold of the MacNeils for perhaps 300 years, but was abandoned in the

Castlebay - with Kisimul Castle on the left, and the CalMac ferry "Clansman" at the pier, Ben Tangaval is in the background

fresh in large chiller trucks direct to the markets.

Today Castlebay is a lively little village, with a comprehensive range of facilities and services, including a new community school complete with swimming pool. *The Feis Bharraigh* takes place for a week each summer, during which visitors and *Bharrachs* participate in the many musical and cultural events which are held.

There are excellent views from **Heaval** (383m), the hill which dominates Castlebay. The statue of the Virgin and Child was sculpted from Carrara marble.

***Dualchas* - Barra Heritage and Cultural Centre** - is next to the school and has interesting displays, old photographs and genealogical information as well as a shop and cafe.

Castlebay Hotel (STB***SMALL HOTEL Tel 01871 810223) overlooks the harbour and has been in the MacLeod family for three generations - pleasant rooms, excellent local seafood and the lively Castlebay Bar.

Also above the harbour, the **Craigard Hotel** (STB***SMALL HOTEL Tel 01871 810200) has recently been fully renovated and offers comfortable rooms and good food.

Facing the Atlantic Ocean at Halaman Bay, the **Isle of Barra Hotel** (STB***HOTEL Tel 01871 810383) is in a dramatic location - the rooms and restaurant have stunning sea views, and the beach is on the doorstep.

View from Heaval over Castlebay and the "Bishop's Isles"

Leaving Castlebay on the ferry - Heaval in background

"The Street" Castlebay

Martin Lawrence

ISLE OF BARRA - *BARRAIGH*

Traigh Mhor - the Cocklestrand - from the south-east

The east coast of Barra is rugged with rocky bays, some with small sandy beaches and low cliffs. The sheltered inlet at Northbay has some of Barra's few trees - excellent places to find migrants in Spring and Autumn. Several passerine species breed here. There is a statue of St Barr on an islet on the loch as well as a modern collage of the saint made with sea shells on the nearby St Barr's Church. The **Northbay Inn** is a good place to meet some local people, or have a snack.

The north-east of the island is quite different in character with expansive flat sandy beaches, backed by sand dunes and machair. **Barra Airport** is unique in that it uses the large flat expanse of *Traigh Mhor*, or the Cocklestrand, as its runways. The tearoom in the terminal is open seven days a week all year.

Operations are dependent on the tide, but the Canadian-built **Twin Otter** aircraft which are used are eminently suitable for the job. There are daily flights to Glasgow and Benbecula. at variable times. The beach is also the source of the wonderful

cockles which may be found on local menus.

There is a new **ro-ro car ferry** route between Aid Mhor near the airport and Eriskay. Substantial new terminals have been constructed at each end and the ferry operates several times per day.

Most of the north of the island is machair, grazed by cattle, while the hay meadows are a refuge for the Corncrake, which may be heard calling here in Summer. The wild flowers in this area are particularly magnificent, especially the **Primroses** of early Summer which carpet the machair and road verges in a sea

Twin Otter landing at Barra Airport

Earsary and east coast bays, Muldoanich in the background

Mosaic of St Barr at Northbay

Northbay from the north-west

of yellow blossoms. Later the machair becomes a riot of whites, yellows, blues, reds and greens as the large variety of wild flowers come into bloom.

Sound of Barra and South Uist from Scurrival

Carpet of Primroses at Eoligarry

Traigh Eais and Traigh Mhor from Dun Scurrival - looking south down the west coast

Cille Bharra (NF704074) overlooks Eoligarry and is said to be dedicated to **St Barr** or Finbar, of Cork, whose feast day is 27th September, although the church may also have connections to St Brendan. None of the three buildings visible appear earlier than 12th century, but it is likely that the original foundation was much earlier, perhaps 7th century.

A very interesting and unusual grave slab was taken to Edinburgh in 1865 (it is now in the NMS), which has a Celtic cross on one side and a runic inscription to Thorgerth, Steiner's daughter. A replica of this 10th or 11th century stone is in the North Chapel along with three 16th century tombstones, probably of MacNeils.

The door on the north wall of the church has inward-sloping door jambs and windows similar to early Irish churches, strengthening its founder's probable Irish provenance.

The graveyard is still in current use and has an interesting range of memorials, from very ancient to modern. The author Compton MacKenzie, of *Whisky Galore* fame, who lived on Barra from 1935-1945, is buried here.

To the east of the church, ***Traigh Cille Bharra*** is another vast expanse of sand at low tide, stretching to the tidal island of Orosay. It is backed by the fertile machair plain of Eoligarry and Saltinish.

Eoligarry crofting township from the south-east

Ben Scurrival from Dun Scurrival

Dun Scurrival (NF695081) is dramatically situated on a rugged 50m hillock with stunning views over the west coast, *Traigh Scurrival* and the Sound of Barra. Parts of the walls and of the intramural galleries are visible. This Iron Age fort is one of several similar structures on Barra and the Bishop's Isles. Sites of such buildings are often indicated by the place name "Borve" from ON *borg* - castle.

Cille Bharra interior with Eoligarry in the background

Although few of these sites have been excavated it seems that many were occupied over a long period, from their original construction in the Iron Age right through to early Norse times. *Dun Cuier* (NF664034), a broch which overlooks Allasdale beach, was excavated in the 1950's and has now been shown to have been reused over a long period.

There is an "aisled wheelhouse" dating from the early centuries AD inland near **Allasdale** (NF677022) which has outbuildings and an associated souterrain. This house is unusual in that most such dwellings in the Western Isles have been found in machair areas. This house sits at the top of a very attractive valley, well above the machair.

Cille Bharra doorway

Barra Golf Course is nearby on *Aird Greian*. This unusual nine-hole course has fences around the greens to keep the sheep out! There are also great views to admire when you are looking for your balls among all the bits of sheep's wool.

Allasdale from Beinn Mhartainn - "Seal Bay"

Traigh Cille Bharra and the Sound of Orosay

View south over west coast from Greian Head

The west coast of Barra is a series of curvaceous sandy beaches, backed by dunes and machair, interspersed by rugged headlands. From **Greian Head** (NF658047), above the Golf Course, with its abandoned WWII radio post, there is a particularly fine view southwards. A rough track leads to the top of the hill.

There are several pleasant walks in the area. *Beinn Mhartainn* (244m NF664021), overlooking the attractive township of Borve, offers outstanding views. Above Craigston an old thatched cottage (*Dubhairidh* G - The Dark Sheiling) has been renovated (NF673014) and is open to visitors in the summer.

Further up the hill to the north, the large and apparently undisturbed mound of *Dun Bharpa* Neolithic chambered cairn (NF672019) is prominent. Several kerbstones are still standing, and the entrance passage can be seen, facing down the valley. There is another chambered cairn (NF677012) further up towards the saddle of the valley.

The beaches of **Allasdale**, *Traigh Hamara*, *Traigh Tuath* and **Halaman Bay** all have their own character. Whether on a calm summer's evening, or during an equinoctial storm, the scene is constantly changing, dynamic, yet peaceful. The beach at Allasdale, or "Seal Bay", is an especially popular place for seals to hail out, and thus also for viewing them.

A coastal walk along the cliffs from **Cleit to Suideachan** follows an old path and affords especially good views over the west of the island, and towards South Uist.

Borve takes its name from the ruined broch, *Dun na Cille* (NF647016), at the head of a small geo, *Port na Cille*. In the adjacent graveyard there are scant ruins of a little chapel, *Cille Bhrianain* (dedicated to St Brendan). A short standing stone is prominent near the gate onto the machair, which in Summer is a sea of wild flowers. Many waders breed here and Oystercatchers are particularly common.

Traigh Tuath and Abhainn Mor, Borve

Dun Bharpa chambered cairn from the west

There is a fine walk south to **Doirlinn Head**, and then to the top of **Ben Tangaval** (333m NL638991) from Halaman Bay. *Dun Ban* (G White Fort) (NF631003) is another ruined galleried broch-type building, in a dramatic clifftop location. There is an excellent view from the top of the hill.

Dun MhicLeoid with mist in evening light

Dun MhicLeoid (erroneously called Sinclair Castle in the 19th century - NL648996) is on a small island on Loch Tangusdale. This tower was originally three stories high and measures about 3.x2.5m internally, with walls about 1.5m thick. St Columba's Well lies near the loch, marked by some white stones. Watch out for Otters here.

Summer sunset over Halaman Bay

Dun Ban, near Doirlinn Head

Sound of Vatersay and causeway from the War Memorial - Allt Chrisal is on the far right above the new road

VATERSAY (ON *Vatrs-oy* - Wet or Watery Island?) was joined to Barra by a causeway in 1990. During the building of the new road very interesting archaeology came to light, mostly in the small valley of *Allt Chrisal* (NL643977), a burn which runs off Ben Tangaval.

From about 3400 to 1800BC there was a settlement on two levelled areas just above the road. Pottery, flint tools and a saddle quern were found, as were several stone burial cists. About 400m east, a small heel-shaped chambered cairn may have been the communal burial tomb for the settlement.

Further up the valley there is a small circular stone hut, which is probably from the "Beaker" period, as nearby a small cist had a nearly intact beaker in it.

The most dramatic building is the **Iron Age wheelhouse**, which lies up the slope to the west of the stream. The substantial walls, piers and central fireplace can all be made out. This house is unusual, as apart from the one at Allasdale, most such houses so far found in the Western Isles have been built into sand dunes, not free-standing as here.

The most recent occupation in the area was in the 18th century, when a blackhouse and associat-

Heel-shaped Neolithic chambered cairn east of Allt Chrisal

Neolithic settlement site, Allt Chrisal

Iron Age roundhouse, Allt Chrisal

ed outbuildings were built near the Neolithic house, but only inhabited for perhaps 40 years, because of a plague of rats from a wrecked ship.

On the north side of Vatersay, **Dun a' Chaolais** is a large ruined broch which commanded the Sound of Vatersay. The road leads eastwards to sheltered **Vatersay Bay** with its lovely sands. On the west side, **Bagh Siar** was the site of the wreck of the emigrant ship, *Annie Jane* in 1853, bound for Quebec. Nearly 400 were drowned, and there is a memorial to the disaster above the beach.

The Vatersay crofting township was established in the early 20th century after "land raids" resulted in the area being divided into crofts. There are good views northwards over Vatersay from **Dun Vatersay** (NL626947) and over Sandray and **Bagh a'Deas** from **Heillanish** (NL633935).

On the east side, at Uineasain (NL665957), the ruined chapel of **Cille Bhrainain** is on a small knoll above a lovely sandy beach facing Castlebay. There is a very fine beach at **Caragrich** on the way to this chapel site.

Vatersay crofting township, Vatersay Bay and Heaval in the background

Bagh a'Deas, overlooking the Sound of Sandray, Vatersay

Dun a'Chaolais Broch, overlooking the Sound of Vatersay, Vatersay

Bagh Siar, where the "Annie Jane" came ashore in 1853

"Annie Jane" memorial, 1880

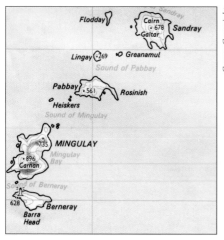

Sandray from Heillanish, Vatersay

The string of islands to the south of Barra was known as the **Bishop's Isles** because during Norse times they were part of the Bishopric Estate. Each is different, with its own character, although all have been uninhabited since the early 20th century.

SANDRAY (ON *Sandr-oy* - Sandy Island) is named for its huge sand dunes on the east coast below Carnach. There is a galleried dun unusually situated at about 100m (NL637913) on the south east ridge of *Cairn Galtar* (207m), and a chapel, *Cille Bhrighde* (NL652919) next to the old settlement site, which is now buried by sand.

PABBAY (ON *Papa-oy* - Irish Monk or Culdee's Island) has a beautiful white sandy beach on the east side, at *Bagh Ban*. The settlement was inland from this, and extensive ruins remain. A small mound nearby has cross-inscribed stones, and may be the site of the chapel. An unusual **inscribed stone**, with a Celtic cross and Pictish symbols used to stand here. On the slope above an Iron Age house similar to those at Bosta on Great Bernera lies excavated, while there is a small, but well preserved galleried dun, *Dunan Ruadh* (G Red Fort NL613877) facing across the Sound of Pabbay to Sandray.

MINGULAY (ON *Mikil-ey* - Muckle or Big Island) is the largest of the Bishop's Isles. The high cliffs up to 215m high on the west side, with spectacular caves, stacks and precipices, are home to many breeding seabirds in summer. There is a 150m nat-

Iron Age house, Pabbay

Pictish symbol stone, Pabbay

Bagh Ban, Pabbay - a beautiful white sandy beach on the east side

Biulacraig and Bagh na h-Aoineig, Mingulay

Mingulay Bay from Aneir

ural arch at *Gumanul.* The best view is from seaward, but only rarely do conditions allow a close approach.

The main settlement's ruined blackhouses, field walls, cultivation strips and a burial ground lie above Mingulay Bay. A chapel, dedicated to St Columba, is now engulfed by sand. The large and incongruous **Chapel House** was built in 1898, but is now unstable, while the **Schoolhouse**, built in the 1880's, is in good repair.

There are good views from **Macphee's Hill** in the north (224m), **Hecla** (219m) in the south and the highest hill, **Carnan** (273m).

BERNERAY (ON *Bjornr-oy* - Bjorn's Island), or **Barra Head**, is the most southerly of the Western Isles. Its dramatic 190m cliffs are topped by Barra Head lighthouse at *Sron an Duine* (G - Fort Headland). The remains of an Iron Age dun at the lighthouse protect a small area surrounded by rocks, right on the edge of the cliffs.

The lighthouse was first lit in 1833 and went automatic in 1980. Barra Head was the way-point for sailing ships west-bound for the USA and Canada, which is one of the reasons of the construction of the light-house.

There is another dun, **Dun**

Briste (NL548806), on the north-west tip of the island. The landing place is on the north-east side below the old settlement. It is only exposed to the east, **"Shelter Rock"** protecting it from the tide and the swell from other airts. There is an old graveyard to the east of Maclean's Point, but nothing remains of the chapel which once stood there.

Barra Head lighthouse

Barra Head from the west. Dun Briste is on the left, Skate Point and Sron an Duin and the lighthouse are in the centre

ST KILDA (ON *Skjoldr* - shield) is a fascinating and beautiful group of islands of volcanic origin 66km WNE of North Uist which was formed by volcanic action about 60 million years ago. It is one of the ultimate destinations for island lovers. The main island is **Hirta** (ON *Hirtir* - deer), which was populated from at least 1850BC until 1930, when it was evacuated. Today the National Trust for Scotland owns the group. A Warden and researchers as well as visitors are present in Summer, and the Missile Range radar station staff all year.

Village Bay from Conachair

"The Street", Village Bay

Village Bay, on the east side, is sheltered from all but easterlys. "The Street" was built in 1860, and the ruined blackhouses behind about 1830, replacing earlier houses which were con-

sidered too primitive. The hillsides are dotted with nearly 1,300 "cleitan" which were used to wind-dry and store birds, fish, dung, hay and peats, preserve eggs and to protect lambs.

Three chapel sites are recorded but nothing now remains. Christ's Church was in the grave yard, St Columba's to the west of the village, and St Brendan's below Ruaival. A Viking female burial was also discovered, but no evidence still survives.

The steep hills offer exhilarating walks which are rewarded by dramatic views, if the tops are clear. Hirta tends to produce its own weather! The main hills are **Oiseval** (290m), **Conachair** (426m). and **Mullach Mor**

(361m). The jagged island of **Dun** protects Village Bay from the south and west. It is home to huge numbers of Puffins in the Summer, and has a ruined dun on its south eastern tip. **Soay** is separated from Hirta by the narrow Sound of Soay with Soay Stac and Stac Biorach in between.

Cleitan are drystone sheds

About 7km to the north-east, **Boreray**, **Stac an Armin** and **Stac Lee** rise steeply from the sea. They are part of the rim of the huge volcano that was here

"The Street", Village Bay, with houses, cleitan and walls

Soay Sheep, Village Bay

Stac an Armin, Boreray and Stac Lee from the south-west

nearly 60m years ago. Together these stacks host the world's largest gannetry with over 60,000 pairs nesting. St Kilda is one of the world's largest seabird colonies with well over 250,000 breeding pairs of all species.

The **St Kildan Wren**, a sub-species, may be seen around the Village area, but seems to prefer the Puffin areas to breed. Their shrill calls make them easy to spot in the old stonework.

A boat trip round Hirta and the stacks during the breeding season is an unforgettable spectacle. The jagged cliffs, lush grassy slopes, thousands of seabirds, and above all the sheer scale of the place can only be described as awe-inspiring.

The St Kildans survived by using Nature's bounty to the full, harvesting thousands of Gannets, Puffins and Fulmars every year. They also kept the primitive Soay Sheep, and later Black-face Sheep. Although there would have been plenty of fish available, it did not feature much in the people's diet - perhaps they preferred it after processing!

Underwater, St Kilda is a sub-aqua diver's paradise, as the volcanic rocks erode into wonderful submerged shapes and caves. The clarity of the water means that visibility is often exceptional, while divers may be accompanied by curious Seals or Puffins.

Many of these offshore islands may be visited with **Sea Trek**. Telephone 01851 672464 or www.seatrek.co.uk

Stac an Armin and Gannets from the south-west

Sound of Soay

Soay from Mullach Mor

The Flannan Islands at sunset from Gallan Head, West Lewis

The **FLANNAN ISLANDS** (after the 8th century St Flann) are situated about 33km WNW of Gallan Head on Lewis. Also known as the **Seven Hunters,** they are another bird paradise in summer, with large numbers of breeding seabirds, including many Puffins, Fulmars, and a small gannetry as well as Storm and Leach's Petrels.

The lighthouse was first lit in 1899 but on 15th December 1900 all three keepers were somehow

lost, perhaps because of being washed away by extremely large waves piling up at the West Landing. The national press had a field day out of it, and the mystery has never really been solved. It has been automatic since 1971, and has now been converted to electric power with a large bank of photocells ranged along the south side.

On *Eilean Mor*, below the lighthouse there is a small stonebuilt chapel, dedicated to **St Flann,**

and on the western headland a series of bothies *(Bothain Chlann 'ic Phaill)* attributed to the Clan MacPhail. There are remains of a possible domestic building on the top of *Eilean Tighe*. Both of these islands have plenty of lush grass and wild flowers in summer.

The gannetry is on the south end of *Roareim*, and should not be closely approached. Between *Roareim* and *Eilean a'Ghobha* there are rock stacks and natural arches eroded into fantastical shapes which can be explored by inflatible if calm.

Landing on *Eilean Mor* is possible at either the east or west landings, while all of the other islands are easily accessible in fine weather. Minke and Pilot Whales, as well as Risso's and other Dolphins frequent this area.

St Flann's Chapel (8th century) and the lighthouse (late 19th century)

West Landing where the keepers may have been lost in December 1900

The lamproom

The **MONACH ISLANDS** (G *Manach* - monks) are about 10km off the west of North Uist. They consist of a series of small sandy islands and low skerries. Legend has it that up to the 16th century a sandbank connected the islands to North Uist, until a huge storm swept the sand away.

The islands are also known as **HEISKER** (ON *Heisker* - Bright skerry), due no doubt to their appearance on a sunny day. The outermost is **Shillay** or *Heisker nam Manach*, where the monks traditionally had to maintain a light. The lighthouse was established in 1864, but has been disused since 1942. A small new light has recently been built here.

Ceann Ear (G East Island) was also known as *Heisker nan Cailleach* due to the nunnery there which may have been established in the 13th century. At low tide *Ceann Ear*, *Shivinish* and *Ceann Iar* are joined by sand bars.

Today the islands are a National Nature Reserve. The undisturbed machair has a particularly rich flora here. About 10,000 **Grey Seals** now come ashore here each autumn to have their pups and mate, making it one of the largest such colonies in the world. Their dung helps fertilise the machair where they have been hauled out. Barnacle Geese also overwinter on the islands.

From seaward on a dull day the Monachs present a forbidding air, with sea breaking on the many rocks and skerries. All of

Shillay lighthouse - disused since 1942 - a new smaller light was lit in 1997

the area in the vicinity is a maze of skerries and sandbanks, but navigable with care. The best anchorage is under the lighthouse at Shillay, where there is a jetty.

Many Waders, Terns, Eider Ducks, Shelducks and Fulmars breed on the islands, which also hold a very large number of **Black Guillemots** which especially like the storm beaches.

Shells and pebbles, Shillay

Shillay and the Monach Islands from the south on a rough day

The shore below the lighthouse, Shillay

Puffins and Thrift - overlooking Sgeildige and Fianuis, Rona

RONA (ON *Hraun-oy* - island with boulder-strewn ground) is a small isolated island about 70km NNE of the Butt of Lewis. The northern *(Fianuis)* and south-western *(Sceapull)* peninsulas

St Ronan's "Oratory"

are quite rough, with bare rock and storm beaches, but the rest of the island is covered with luxuriant grass and wild flowers.

The **hermitage** is one of the oldest complete Celtic sites in Scotland and is said to have been founded by **St Ronan** in the 7th or 8th century. The **"oratory"** seems to be the oldest part of the chapel, which is surrounded by an oval earth and stone wall. There are a number of cross-inscribed and cross-shaped grave markers which may date from the 7th to 9th and from the 12th or 13th centuries. The best known one, said to be St Ronan's own, is in the **Ness Heritage Centre**, Lewis.

A complex group of domestic buildings to the west of the chapel was occupied until the early 18th century. There are sub-rectangular living rooms, small oval side chambers with corbelled roofs, and porches, as well as byres, a granary and extensive field walls and f*eannagan*. It seems that up to five families lived here, excess people going to Lewis, and resettlement also coming from there.

The island is a National Nature Reserve on account of its importance as a seabird and seal breeding area. There are large numbers of breeding Puffins, Guillemots, Kittiwake and Fulmars, as well as both Leach's and Storm Petrels. In autumn up to 8,000 Grey Seals come ashore to calve. The lush grass of summer is partly a consequence of their dung.

Landing is possible in several places, at *Geodh' a'Stoth* in the east, *Sgeildige* in the north-west, or in several places on the south coast. Although small and remote, Rona has a character all of its own and its few visitors find that the experience is more than worth the trip.

Toa Rona and Geodh' a'Sgoth

Feannagan (lazy beds) above the settlement site, Rona

SULA SGEIR (ON *Sula sker* - Gannet Skerry) is a small narrow rock, about 17km SW of Rona. In summer it is home to large numbers of Gannets, Guillemots, Razorbills, Shags Fulmars and Puffins. Both Storm and Leach's Petrels also nest here. There is a sheltered anchorage at **Geodha a'Phuill Bhain**, where landing is not too difficult in settled weather.

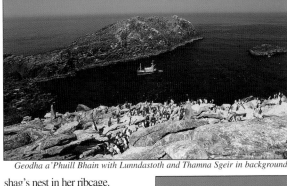

Geodha a'Phuill Bhain with Lunndastoth and Thamna Sgeir in background

Each August the **Men of Ness** come to "harvest" up to 2,000 *gugas*, the plump young Gannets which have not quite fledged. The birds are salted on the island, and are considered a delicacy by everyone from Ness. *Gugas* can grace tables all over the world. Despite the cull, the Gannet population remains stable at about 9,000 pairs. The Gannetry covers the whole southern end of the island.

shag's nest in her ribcage.

The hard gneiss rock splits into long pieces, which are excellent for building bothies and cairns, but the hard rough boulders and sharp rocks make for tough walking. The sea has burrowed right through the southern part of the island in a series of interconnected and spectacular caves which can be explored in calm weather by inflatable.

Guillemots and Gannets

Although seemingly very inhospitable to humans, there is a ruined stone bothy called *Tigh Beannaichte* (Blessed House) on the east headland Sgeir an Teampall. St Ronan's sister, Brenhilda, is supposed to have stayed here for some time, leaving him on Rona, only to be found dead in a bothy with a

The small lighthouse on the south end at *Sron na Lice* is regularly damaged by the huge seas which break right over the rock during Atlantic storms. Despite this there is a surprising amount of vegetation, the Thrift being especially luxuriant and colourful in June, which is probably the best month to visit.

Bealach at t-Suidhe from cave

Tigh Beannaichte - ruined bothy

The south end - Sron na Lice with its small lighthouse

Approaching the Shiants from the east

The **SHIANT ISLANDS** (G *Na h-Eileanan Seunta* - The Enchanted Islands) lie between Skye and Lewis at the south end of the Minch and are about 18km east of Scalpay. The rocks here are volcanic, and at 60m years, very young by Hebridean standards.

The dolerite columns on the north side of *Garbh Eilean* (G Rough Isle) are over 100m tall and about 2m across. Similar to those at Staffa and the Giant's Causeway, they were caused by the slow cooling of volcanic rocks deep underground. In some places the basalt is overlain by Jurassic mudstone, which weathers to form much more fertile soil than elsewhere in the Western Isles.

The previously inhabited and cultivated areas of *Airighean a'Baigh* and *Airighean na h-Annaid* on *Eilean Garbh* and most of the top of *Eilean Mhuire* (G The Virgin's Island) are unusually fertile land for this reason. *Feannagan* may still be made out in these areas.

Apart from the 19th century house and adjacent ruins on *Eilean an Tighe* (G - House Island) there is substantial other evidence of human occupation. It seems that the islands were inhabited up until the late 18th century, when changes in land ownership and society made the old way of life no longer viable.

There are several possible chapel sites. The first may have been dedicated to St Columba and have been on the west side of *Eilean Garbh*, perhaps at *Airighean na h-Annaid*, as the name *"Annaid"* means Old Church. There is also evidence of a more recent church, dedicated to the Virgin, near the present cottage.

During excavations on the farmstead on *Eilean an Tighe* an interesting **round stone** with a cross surrounded by a circle was found. This type of stone is common in Ireland, but unusual in Scotland, and was probably buried by the builders for good luck, but must have come from a much earlier church site.

Another interesting find was a **gold torc** which was dredged up by some Scalpay scallop fishermen south-west of the islands. This beautiful object dates from perhaps 1200BC, and while similar such torcs have turned up elsewhere in UK, this is by far the furthest north. It is possible to speculate endlessly about the provenance of such a find, and whether it got there by shipwreck, or as a votive offering.

The Shiants are a major seabird breeding ground due to their location next to good feeding grounds and lack of

Eilean Tighe - modern cottage and ancient settlement site

predators, except for Black Rats. Huge numbers of Puffins breed in burrows on the slopes of *Garbh Eilean*, as well as significant numbers of Guillemots, Razorbills, Fulmars, Kittiwakes, Shags, Gulls and Great Skuas. Although St Kilda has more Puffins, the sheer density on the Shiants is greater.

The Sound of Shiant or **Sruth na Fear Gorm** is said to be inhabited by the *"Blue Men of the Minch"*, who must be treated with the greatest respect by mariners. Certainly the strong tides, uneven seabed and many hazards make the area dangerous in bad conditions.

The offshore rocks and stacks to the west of the Shiants are called the **Galtachean** (which may derive from ON *Goltr* - boar). Their basalt columns are beautiful on a calm day, but fearsome when the sea is rough. The best landing is on the shingle and boulder beach at **Mol Mor** on the east side of the isthmus, between *Eilean Tighe* and *Garbh Eilean*.

Massive dolerite columns on the north face of Garbh Eilean - 150m high

Cross-incised stone

Adam Nicholson

NMS

Golden torc from the Minch

Eilean Tighe and Garbh Eilean from Eilean Mhuire

Garbh Eilean and Mol Mor from Eilean Tighe

Dolerite columns on Garbh Eilean

"Isle of Lewis" at Stornoway ferry terminal

The Western Isles may appear to be remote and isolated from the map, but they are very easy to get to by both air and sea. There are good connections by air from three Scottish airports, while ferries run from Ullapool in Wester Ross, Uig on Skye and Oban. Travel to these ports is facilitated by good roads as well as bus and rail links which tie in with the ferry times.

SEA The main ferry operator is **Caledonian MacBrayne**, known universally as *CalMac*, whose ferries make regular sailings to Stornoway from Ullapool, Tarbert and Lochmaddy from Uig and Castlebay and Lochboisdale from Oban. *There are no Sunday sailings to Lewis, Harris or North Uist.*

CalMac offer Island Hopscotch and Island Rover tickets which offer substantial savings.

Caledonian Macbrayne, The Ferry Terminal, Gourock PA19 1QP
Tel 01475 650100,
Fax 01475 637607.
Online bookings and timetables on their website www.calmac.co.uk.

There are local offices at Stornoway, Tel 01851 702361, Tarbert, Tel 01859 502444, Lochmaddy, Tel 01876 500337 Lochboisdale, Tel 01878 700288.

AIR There are direct daily services operated by **British Airways** partner carriers, into **Stornoway (SYY)** from Edinburgh, Glasgow and Inverness, **Benbecula (BEB)** from Glasgow and **Barra (BRR)** from Glasgow. as well as flights to Stornoway and Benbecula from Inverness by **Highland Airways**. Regular internal flights also link Stornoway, Benbecula and Barra. *There are no Sunday flights.*

British Airways 24/7
Bookings Tel 0845 77 333 77
Information 0870 55 111 55
Other enquiries 0845 77 999 77
www.britishairways.com

Highland Airways, Stornoway Island Hopper Service
Tel 01851 701282
www.highlandairways.co.uk

HOLIDAY OPERATORS
There are a number of travel companies which offer independent travel advice and bookings to the Western Isles. There is also a wide range of specialist operators offering organised tours, cruises and activities. For the latest information see the current WITB brochure, or telephone WITB for advice.

HEBRIDEAN HOPSCOTCH is a local group which offers great value car touring packages which include all car ferry charges as well as 3 to 14 nights Dinner, Bed and Breakfast in the hotels of your choice. Flexibility, ease of booking and quality of service ensure that this one of the best ways to enjoy a visit to the Western Isles.

Hebridean Hopscotch Holidays, 11 James Street, Stornoway, Isle of Lewis HS1 2QN
Tel 01851 706600,
Fax 01851 703900,
www.calahotels.com
kenneth@calahotels.com

For other Travel Operators please see the current WITB brochure

WESTERN ISLES TOURIST BOARD (WITB)
The local Tourist Board produces a very informative annual brochure with details of transport, accommodation, activities and events. Its websites are also excellent for planning.

Western Isles Tourist Board, 26 Cromwell Street, Stornoway, Isle of Lewis HS1 1DD
Tel 01851 703088
Fax 01851 705244
www.witb.co.uk
stornowaytic@witb.ossian.net

Getting out and about is all part of a visit to the Western Isles. This Guide describes the huge number of places to explore, but the visitor must be able to reach them in the first place. Distances in the islands can be deceptively large - it is nearly 200km (130 miles) from one end to the other! The roads are quiet, except during "rush times" in Stornoway, with little heavy traffic. Most are excellent, but many are still single track, so please take care.

The empty roads, and generally flat country make for excellent cycling - but beware there are steep hills, and the wind can be strong. Many people take their bikes with them. Walking is also an option, but watch out for vehicles on the single track roads. Getting lifts is also no problem - people will often stop and ask if you really want to walk!

LOCAL TRAVEL INFORMATION
The Tourist Information Offices in Stornoway, Tarbert, Lochmaddy, Lochboisdale and Castlebay are the best places to seek the latest timetables and information on travel operators. The annual WITB brochure has details of members offering travel services.

BUSES
Local bus services connect most of the main settlements, as well as with inter-island ferries. The "Skye and Western Isles Travel Guide" gives details of all of these routes and times.

INTER-ISLAND TRAVEL
There are connecting flights between Stornoway, Benbecula and Barra. CalMac operates a vehicle ferry between Harris and North Uist as well as between South Uist and Barra.

CAR AND BIKE HIRE
Independent transport is strongly recommended in order to reach most of the places and sites of interest mentioned in this guide, many of which are "off the beaten trail". A car is virtually essential to those with time limitations, while a bike allows a much more leisurely approach. The ideal is of course to combine the two. There are car and bike hire outlets on all the main islands.

Bicycle and equipment hire available from **Fifty Eight Degrees North**, Adventure Outfitters. Tel 01851 820726 or 01851 672464.
www.58degreesNorth.co.uk

TAXIS, COACH TOURS AND GUIDING SERVICES
Taxis are available in all locations, and are especially useful when catching ferries or flights. Minibus and coach tours are also run by several companies. Guiding is available from qualified Western Isles Tour Guides.

PETROL STATIONS
Apart from in the main centres of population, filling stations tend to be few and far between. Most are closed on Sunday, and while some are open for long hours, others are not. It is best to keep your tank topped up!

TRIPS, CRUISES AND ACTIVITIES
Wildlife cruises to islands, hillwalking and rambling, guided walks, sub aqua, sea kayaking, trout and salmon fishing, riding school, rock climbing and golf are some of the many organised activities on offer. Further information from the TICs, or the current WITB brochure.

For **boat trips and offshore adventure** contact **Sea Trek**.
Tel 01851 672464
www.seatrek.co.uk

To hire **canoes, bicycles and camping equipment** contact **Fifty Eight Degrees North**, Adventure Outfitters. Tel 01851 820726 or 01851 672464.
www.58degreesNorth.co.uk

SHOPPING AND CRAFTS
There are many interesting shops on the islands, which sell locally-produced items, including Harris Tweed, pottery, knitwear, artwork, Lewis chessmen replicas and other crafts. Some are quite remote - so seek them out.

FOOD AND DRINK
There are excellent places to eat and drink throughout the islands. Seafood is especially good here, but all tastes are catered for. Since many establishments are closed on Sundays, or have limited hours, it is always a good idea to phone ahead and book to avoid disappointment. Recommended places to eat are mentioned in the text and there is a list of advertisers on p138-139.

GAELIC CULTURE
No visitor to the Western Isles can fail to notice that the everyday language is Gaelic and not English for many of the inhabitants. There are various events held throughout the islands during the year when visitors can experience Gaelic culture.

ISLE OF LEWIS

Royal Hotel, Cromwell Street, STORNOWAY, Isle of Lewis HS1 2DG
Tel 01851 702109 Fax 01851 702142
royal@calahotels.com
www.calahotels.com
STB**HOTEL 26 bedrooms (26 en-suite) Centrally situated overlooking Castle and Harbour.

Cabarfeidh Hotel, Manor Park, STORNOWAY, Isle of Lewis HS1 2EU
Tel 01851 702604 Fax 01851 705572
cabarfeidh@calahotels.com
www.calahotels.com
STB***HOTEL 46 bedrooms (all en-suite) In quiet area on edge of town, near Castle grounds.

Seaforth Hotel, 9 James Street, STORNOWAY, Isle of Lewis HS1 2QN
Tel 01851 702740 Fax 01851 703900
seaforth@calahotels.com
www.calahotels.com
STB**HOTEL 68 bedrooms (all en-suite) Centrally situated near harbour and shops.

Doune Braes Hotel, CARLOWAY, Isle of Lewis HS2 9AA
Tel 01851 643252   Fax 01851 643435
hebrides@doune-braes.co.uk
www.doune-braes.co.uk
STB***SMALL HOTEL, 11 rooms (all en-suite) fine food served all day, comfortable rooms and a warm welcome.

Galson Farm Guest House, SOUTH GALSON, Isle of Lewis HS2 0SH Tel/Fax 01851 850492
galsonfarm@yahoo.com
www.galsonfarm.freeserve.co.uk
STB****GUEST HOUSE 11 rooms (all en-suite) Guests made very much at home, and memorable home cooking by Dorothy.

Baile-na-Cille Guest House, TIMS-GARRY, Isle of Lewis HS2 9JD
Tel 01851 672242 Fax 01851 672241
randjgollin@compuserve.com
STB**GUEST HOUSE Friendly welcome to visitors, wonderful food. good centre to explore Lewis and Harris from.

ISLE OF HARRIS

Harris Hotel, Tarbert, Isle of Harris HS3 3DL Tel 01859 502154 Fax 01859 502281
c a m e r o n h a r r i s @ b t i n t e r n e t . c o m
www.harrishotel.com

STB**HOTEL 24 bedrooms (15) Island hospitality at its best - a warm welcome, friendly service and excellent food in relaxed surroundings.

Scarista House, Scarista, Isle of Harris HS3 3HX
Tel 01859 550238 Fax 01859 550277
timandpatricia@scaristahouse.com
www.scaristahouse.com
STB****GUEST HOUSE 5 bedrooms (all ensuite)
Traditional comfort and natural skilled cooking in a stunning location with ocean views.

NORTH UIST

Claddach Kirkibost Centre, NORTH UIST HS6 5EP   Tel 01876 580390 Conservatory cafe, local produce and homebaking, open seasonally. Email and Internet facilities. Childcare facilities. Demonstrations & cultural events.

Ardmaree Stores & Lobster Pot Cafe, BERNERAY, North Uist HS7 5BJ
Tel 01876 540288 Licensed cafe and grocery store.

BENBECULA

Stepping Stone Restaurant, BALIVANICH, Benbecula HS7 5LA Tel 01870 603377 Fax 01870 603121
Specialising in seafood and Scottish fayre. Adjacent to Benbecula airport.

Creagorry Hotel, CREAGORRY, Benbecula HS7 5PG Tel 01870 602024 Fax 01870 603108
darkislandhotel@msn.com
www.witb.co.uk/links/isleshotels.htm
STB*HOTEL, 16 bedrooms (all en-suite) Conveniently located old-established hotel.

Dark Island Hotel, LINICLATE, Benbecula HS7 5PJ Tel 01870 603030 Fax 01870 602347
darkislandhotel@msn.com
www.witb.co.uk/links/isleshotels.htm
STB**HOTEL, 42 bedrooms (all en-suite) Comfortable rooms and excellent food.

SOUTH UIST

Orasay Inn, LOCHCARNAN, South Uist HS8 5PD Tel 01870 610298 Fax 01870 610390
orasayinn@btinternet.com
www.witb.co.uk/orasayinn.htm

STB**INN, 9 bedrooms (all en-suite) offers comfortable accommodation, and fine "Scottish Natural Cooking", prepared by chef Isobel Graham.

Lochboisdale   Hotel, LOCHBOISDALE, South Uist HS8 5TH   Tel 01878 700332   Fax 01878 700367
hotel@lochboisdale.com
www.lochboisdale.com
STB***HOTEL, 17 bedrooms (all ensuite) Traditional sporting hotel much used by anglers. Non-fishermen equally welcome.

Borrodale Hotel, DALIBURGH, South Uist HS8 5SS Tel 01878 700444 Fax 01878 700446
reception@borrodalehotel.co.uk
www.witb.co.uk/links/isleshotels.htm
STB***SMALL HOTEL, 12 bedrooms (all ensuite), which is also a good place to stay, or to stop for a meal.

Anchorage Restaurant, Ferry Terminal, An t-Ob, HARRIS Tel 01859 520225 Breakfast, lunch, evening meals, snacks and take-aways. Handy for the ferry to North Uist.

ISLE OF BARRA

Castlebay Hotel, CASTLEBAY, Isle of Barra HS9 5XD Tel 01871 810223 Fax 01871 810455
castlebayhotel@aol.com
www.castlebay-hotel.co.uk
STB***SMALL HOTEL 12 bedrooms (all ensuite) overlooks the harbour in MacLeod family for 3 generations - pleasant rooms, excellent local seafood and the lively Castlebay Bar.

Craigard Hotel, CASTLEBAY, Isle of Barra HS9 5XD Tel 01871 810200 Fax 01871 810726
craigard@isleofbarra.com
www.isleofbarra.com/craigard.html
STB***SMALL HOTEL, (7 bedrooms (all ensuite) has recently been fully renovated and offers comfortable rooms and good food.

Isle of Barra Hotel, Tangusdale Beach, Isle of Barra HS9 5XW Tel 01871 810383 Fax 01871 810385
barrahotel@aol.com
www.isleofbarra.com/iob.html
STB***HOTEL 30 bedrooms (all ensuite) is in a dramatic location - the rooms and restaurant have stunning sea views.

The Western Isles have a large range of Visitor Attractions, Tour Organisers, Activities, Shops and Services which are available for the visitor. Those who have supported this publication by taking advertising space are listed below. For further information please see the current Western Isles Tourist Board brochure, or contact any of the businesses listed on these pages.

Sunset at Halaman Bay, Barra

ARTS & CRAFTS

An Lanntair, Arts Centre, Cafe & Shop, Old Town Hall, South Beach, STORNOWAY Tel 01851 703307 Fax 01851 703307
lanntair@sol.co.uk
www.lanntair.com
Regular exhibitions by local, national and international artists, cafe and small but interesting shop.

Anthony Barber, Harbour View Gallery, Port of Ness, LEWIS Tel 01851 810735
ajb@harbourview.freeserve.co.uk
www.abarber.co.uk
Original watercolours, prints and greetings cards by the artist, on sale from his studio and in shops in the islands.

Borgh Pottery, 5 Penny House, Borgh, LEWIS Tel 01851 850345
borghpottery@yahoo.co.uk
www.borghpottery.com
Sue & Alex Blair - unique ceramics and gifts - hand thrown studio pottery. - irresistible shop.

Gisla Woodcraft, Gisla, Uig, LEWIS Tel 01851 672371
carol.macdonald0@talk21.com
www.witb.co.uk/links/gisla.htm
Scottish woods turned by hand into many beautiful, but useful items. Craft shop with interesting gifts.

Island Crafts, Cnoc Aird, GRIMSAY and in Lochmaddy. Tel 01870 602418
Local crafts - "for something original and a little bit different" - local crafts, books, cards, knitwear, etc.

BOOKSHOPS

MacGillivrays, Balivanich,Benbecula HS7 5LA Tel 01870 602525 Fax 01870 602981 The Hebridean gift house - an "Alladin's Cave of quality. Souvenirs, clothing, tweed, books, crafts, fishing tackle, etc. Mail order service.

Roderick Smith Ltd, The Baltic Bookshop, 8-10 Cromwell Street, STORNOWAY Tel 01851 702082 Fax 01851 706644
rsmith@sol.co.uk
www.balticbookshop.co.uk
Excellent selection of local interest, Scottish and general books in the Western Isles' biggest bookshop. Secure online ordering of Western Isles and other books. Also sells newspapers and magazines.

GENEALOGY & LANDSCAPE

Seallam! Visitor Centre, Taobh Tuath, HARRIS Tel 01859 520258
seallam@cs.com
www.seallam.com
People and landscape of the Hebrides, shop, tea/coffee bar. Co Leis Thu? - genealogy research - find out about your Hebridean ancestors. Bill Lawson books as well as an interesting selection of other Hebridean and Scottish, books, CDs, etc.

SEAFOOD

Salar Ltd, The Pier, Lochcarnan, SOUTH UIST Tel 01870 610324
sales@salar.co.uk
www.salar.co.uk
Delicious, award-winning Salar Flaky Smoked Salmon is sold throughout the Western Isles and the UK. It is also available by mail order.

IMAGES & PHOTOGRAPHY

WHB Sutherland, Victoria Street, KIRKWALL, Orkney KW15 1DN Tel 01856 873240 Fax 01856 872141
photolab@orkney.com
www.hebridesimages.co.uk
Digitally-mastered images of the Western Isles and other areas from the Charles Tait collection. Secure online ordering.

Charles Tait photographic, Kelton, St Ola, ORKNEY KW15 1TR Tel 01856 873738 Fax 01856 875313
charles.tait@zetnet.co.uk
www.charles-tait@zetnet.co.uk
Publishers of Guide Books, Postcards and Calendars. Photo Library Western Isles, Orkney and Shetland. Digitally mastered prints available from images in this book.

During the research for this book well over 300 books, periodicals, guides, maps and other publications were consulted as well as many individuals and websites. The author wishes to thank everyone who has been of assistance during his years of wanderings in the Western Isles.

The following bibliography is a distillation of some of the books on the area. Some are essential reading, others depend on personal interests.

One of the best starting places is Hamish Haswell-Smith's book on the Scottish Islands, but then the author is a fellow sea-lover.

Many locally-produced leaflets, guides and small books are available produced by the Tourist Board, Scottish Natural Heritage and other bodies or individuals. In particular the walks leaflets by WITB and SNH are excellent. Bill Lawson produces a very good series of little

books on chapels and genealogy and the various heritage centres and museums also do very useful local guides.

Apart from the Baltic Bookshop in Stornoway, many shops throughout the isles stock local books. The TICs and museums are also good sources of local publications, some of which are free, while others may be charged for.

ESSENTIAL BACKGROUND READING

The Scottish Islands	Hamish Haswell-Smith	Canongate	1996
West Over Sea	DDC Pochin Mould	Acair	1953
A Description of the Western Isles of Scotland circa 1695	Martin Martin	Birlinn	1698
The Archaeology of Skye and the Western Isles	Ian Armit	Edinburgh University Press	1996
Facing the Ocean - The Atlantic and its Peoples	Barry Cunliffe	Oxford	2001
Scotland's Hidden History	Ian Armit	Tempus	1998
The Ancient Monuments of the Western Isles	ed Denys Pringle	HMSO	1994
The Making of the Crofting Community	James Hunter	John Donald	1976
Island Going	Robert Atkinson	Birlinn	1949
An Island Odyssey	Hamish Haswell-Smith	Canongate	1999

GENERAL BOOKS ON THE WESTERN ISLES

Isles of the West	Ian Mitchell	Canongate	1999
The Western Isles - A Postcard Tour, 1 Barra to North Uist	Bob Carnley	MacLean Press	1992
The Western Isles - A Postcard Tour, 2 Harris & Lewis	Bob Carnley	MacLean Press	1993
Lewis & Harris	Francis Thompson	Pevensey	1999
Lewis - The Story of an Island	Christine Macdonald	Acair	1998
Benbecula	Ray Burnett	Mingulay Press	1986
Uists & Barra	Francis Thompson	Pevensey	1999
Road to the Isles, Travellers in the Hebrides 1770-1914	Derek Cooper	MacMillan	1979

HISTORY & ARCHAEOLOGY

The Stone Circles of Britain, Ireland and Brittany	Aubrey Burl	Yale	2000
The Extraordinary Voyage of Pytheas the Greek	Barry Cunliffe	Allen Lane	2001
The Illustrated Life of Columba	John Marsden	Floris Books	1991
The Lewis Chessmen	Neil Stratford	British Museum Press	1997
Somerled and the Emergence of Gaelic Scotland	John Marsden	Tuckwell Press	2000
The Lords of the Isles	Raymond Campbell Paterson	Birlinn	2001
Polly The True Story Behind Whisky Galore	Roger Hutchinson	Mainstream	1990
North Uist	Erskine Beveridge	Birlinn	1911

GUIDE BOOKS

The Western Isles, Innsegall	J Barber & DA Magee	John Donald	1989
Calanais, The Standing Stones	Patrick Ashmore	Urras nan Tursachan	1995
Argyll and the Western Isles	Graham Ritchie & Mary Harman	HMSO	1996
Birdwatching in the Outer Hebrides	Cunningham, Dix & Snow	Saker Press	1995
The Island Blackhouse	Alexander Fenton	Historic Scotland	1978
Scotland Highlands and Islands Handbook	Alan Murphy	Footprint	2001
The Chapels in the Western Isles	Finlay MacLeod	Acair	1997

HISTORY-SCOTTISH CONNECTION

Go Listen to the Crofters	AD Cameron	Acair	1986
From the Land (As an Fhearann)	ed M MacLean & C Carrell	Mainstream	1986
The Lewis Land Struggle	Joni Buchanan	Acair	1996
Who Owns Scotland Now?	Auslan Cramb	Mainstream	1996
Historic Stornoway	EP Dennison & R Coleman	Historic Scotland	1997
The Hebrides at War	Mike Hughes	Canongate	1998
The Companion to Gaelic Scotland	ed Derick S Thomson	Gairm	1994
Times Subject to Tides - The Story of Barra Airport	Roy Calderwood	Kea Publishing	1999

NATURAL HISTORY

The Outer Hebrides - The Shaping of the Islands	Stewart Angus	White Horse Press	1998
The Hebrides	JM & IL Boyd	Collins	1990
Scottish Birds - Culture and Tradition	Robin Hull	Mercat Press	2001
The Landscape of Scotland, A Hidden History	CR Wickham-Jones	Tempus	2001
Plants and People in Ancient Scotland	Camilla & James Dickson	Tempus	2000

ACTIVITIES

Fisher in the West	Eddie Young	Stornoway Gazette	1994
70 Lochs - A Guide to Trout Fishing in South Uist	John Kennedy	John Kennedy	1997
Trout Fishing in Lewis	N MacLeod, E Young	Western Isles Publishing Co	1993
Walking in the Hebrides	Roger Redfern	Cicerone	1998
25 Walks The Western Isles	June Parker	HMSO	1996

OUTLYING ISLANDS

An Isle Called Hirte	Mary Harman	MacLean Press	1997
Mingulay	Ben Buxton	Birlinn	1995
Sea Room An Island Life	Adam Nicolson	Harper Collins	2001
St Kilda	David Quine	Colin Baxter	1995
Sula, The Seabird-Hunters of Lewis	John Beatty	Michael Joseph	1992
St Kilda The Continuing Story of the Islands	ed Meg Buchanan	HMSO	1995
Rona - The Distant Island	Michael Robson	Acair	1991

PHOTOGRAPH BOOKS

Nis Aosmhor - The Photographs of Dan Morrison		Acair	1997
Patterns of the Hebrides	Gus Wylie	Zwemmer	1981
A Poem of Remote Lives - Images of Eriskay 1934	Werner Kissling	Neil Wilson	1997

SEA AND BOATS

The West Highland Galley	Denis Rixson	Birlinn	1998
The Yachtsman's Pilot to the Western Isles	Martin Lawrence	Imray Laurie Norie & Wilson	1996
Birlinn, Longships of the Hebrides	John MacAuley	White Horse Press	1996

STORIES AND FOLKLORE

Stories from South Uist told by Angus MacLennan	trans John L Campbell	Birlinn	1997
Tales from Barra told by the Coddie	Intro & Notes JL Campbell	Birlinn	1992
The Furrow Behind Me told by Angus MacLennan	trans John L Campbell	Birlinn	1997
The Voice of the Bard	Timothy Neat with John MacInnes	Canongate	1999
Seal-Folk and Ocean Paddlers	JM MacAuley	White Horse Press	1998
The Finlay J MacDonald Omnibus	Finlay J MacDonald	Warner	1994
Whisky Galore	Compton MacKenzie	Penguin	1947

MAPS

Ordnance Survey 1:50,000 Landranger maps numbers 8,13,14,18,22 and 31 cover the Western Isles, while the Pathfinder 1:25,000 series covers the same area in 36 sheets. The latest maps have the newer Gaelic place names. The Western Isles Tourist Board also produces a useful map with both new Gaelic and older English place names at a scale of 1:125,000. Also useful is the Ordnance Survey 1:250,000 Travelmaster sheet number 3 "Western Scotland and the Western Isles"

INDEX

Traigh Iar with Clach Mhic Leoid on the horizon